Harold Truscott

THE MUSIC OF
FRANZ SCHMIDT

Volume One:
The Orchestral Music

THE MUSIC OF
FRANZ SCHMIDT

Volume One
THE ORCHESTRAL MUSIC

HAROLD TRUSCOTT

With Personal Recollections by
HANS KELLER

And the 'Autobiographical Sketch' by
FRANZ SCHMIDT

**TOCCATA
PRESS**

First published in 1984 by Toccata Press.
© Harold Truscott and Hans Keller, 1984.
Appendix © the Franz Schmidt Haus, Perchtoldsdorf, 1939;
  translation © Toccata Press, 1984.

Music examples drawn by Andrew Vores

British Library Cataloguing in Publication Data

Truscott, Harold
  The music of Franz Schmidt.
  Vol. 1 : The orchestral music
  1. Schmidt, Franz
  I. Title   II. Keller, Hans   III. Schmidt, Franz
  780'.92'4   ML410.S2614

  ISBN 0-907689-11-6 (cased edition)
  ISBN 0-907689-12-4 (paperback edition)

Set in 11 on 12 point Baskerville
  by Alan Sutton Publishing, Gloucester.
Printed by Nene Litho, and bound by Woolnough Binding,
  Wellingborough.

Contents

List of Illustrations

PERSONAL RECOLLECTIONS: OSKAR ADLER'S AND MY OWN

Hans Keller

As a composer, conductor, piano virtuoso, chamber-musical pianist, and string-quartet cellist, Franz Schmidt was the most complete musician I have come across in my life. As a composer, and at a stage in the history of musical creativity when abstract considerations had begun to interfere with concrete creative thought, he only wrote what he heard – and one had to know him in order to appreciate how clearly he heard the most complex textures, in which his inner ear would balance and blend colours more distinctly and clearly than does the outer ear of many a (mis-) leading quartet player or conductor. And though you could not call him a professional conductor, the acuteness of his outer ear turned his conducting into unforgettable experiences.

When I talk about 'the most complete musician', I am talking about a type of musician no longer extant: under the influence of the inescapable assault on our ears which contemporary civilization confronts us with, our power of aural concentration and our quality of listening have deteriorated to an extent which, *pro tempore*, make the birth of a Franz Schmidt impossible. What am I talking about? About the simple fact that he knew, and remembered, all music. Whatever you raised, whether it was a point about a tricky passage in the Matthew Passion or John Passion, in a late Beethoven quartet, in any of the later Haydn symphonies, in a Bruckner symphony and, yes, in Schoenberg's *Transfigured Night* or *Gurrelieder*, he would jump up, waddle across to the piano, and play the passage in question in an instant, perfect piano arrangement, stressing the inner part you happened to be talking about. Once I noticed that this was the case, I tried my unsuccessful best to challenge his memory, to raise a point about an unwell-known masterpiece; I can't remember a

single occasion on which he failed to play me the passage in
question more precisely than I had remembered it.

At the same time, what was most overwhelming in one's
experience of his musical personality was the sheer intensity of
his imagination. As a conductor and as a player, he never gave
two performances of the same work without making one a
drastic variation of the other. No wonder Mahler insisted on
Schmidt's playing the cello solos in the Vienna
Philharmonic – even though the official principal cellist was
Friedrich Buxbaum,[1] the cellist of the Rosé Quartet, with
which body I heard Schmidt play, as a pianist, the 'Trout'
Quintet and, as a cellist, the Schubert C major, where he did,
of course, play the second cello – fortunately: the imagination
he pumped into the notorious second-cello passages in the
slow movement had to be heard to be believed, especially
when they turned into something entirely different in the next
performance.

But at his greatest as a chamber-musician he was not with
the Rosé Quartet, whose approach to music differed from his
own, but in both his weekly quartet sessions with Oskar Adler
(Schoenberg's first quartet leader and first teacher) and, as a
pianist, his duo with Oskar Adler, which gave about one
recital a year, to a packed hall; their broadcasts, too, were few
and far between. For they did take chamber music seriously,
and confined it to the chamber, where a carefully selected
audience was admitted to their regular sessions, which invariably comprised at least four masterpieces; only when a
Schmidt quartet was being studied were most members of the
select audience not admitted. My own experience was not
confined to that of a listener; Adler, who was my teacher too,
actually introduced me to Schmidt as a quartet player. I was
far too nervous to play the Haydn quartet Adler selected as I
wanted to, what with Schmidt sitting opposite me, the second
fiddler, and the cream of Vienna's musicians listening; nevertheless, as I subsequently heard from Adler, Schmidt foresaw
my future pretty precisely.

For the rest, my personal recollections of Schmidt are

[1] *Cf.* Schmidt's *Autobiographical Sketch*, pp. 176–178.

Schmidt and his second wife, Margarethe (*née* Jirasek), with Oskar Adler on Perchtoldsdorf Heath in 1932. Besides being Schmidt's doctor and partner in chamber music, Adler was also an author of books on astrological and mystical themes.

largely identical with many of Adler's own, to whom I can hand over at this stage in my introduction, for an odd reason: I have in my possession a copy of a letter which Oskar Adler wrote to Schmidt's widow, and in which he recounted as many biographical details as he could muster. In none of the books or articles or chapters on Franz Schmidt I have seen was this biographical information used; it would certainly have prevented many of those factual mistakes with which the literature on Schmidt abounds. It may well be that Adler left me the copy of this letter together with other countless documents and scores; in any case, I herewith submit my translation of its salient passages, which will throw new light on the life and work of a master whom even many a dictionary entry factually misrepresents.

'My dearest Mrs Schmidt,

'Below, I give you a disorderly account of some of my recollections of Franz Schmidt, with whom I was linked by a more than 20-year-old friendship and a common musical experience which flowed from our regularly playing quartets together. My account is inevitably unsystematic, for I have to write down what passes through my head. These experiences of our quartet-playing were almost "not of this world"; they were like a service to God, a fact on which we wholly agreed without ever talking about it. My recollections belong to my most valuable experiences during the time between the beginning of the First World War and my departure, with my wife, for England in 1938.

'We first met in the hospitable house of Mrs Saphir . . . whose oldest son, Fritz Saphir, was a cello pupil of Franz Schmidt's. . . . At the time, Fritz Saphir was cellist in my quartet and often enthused about me to Schmidt. But Schmidt was suspicious: "What sort of a fiddler can that be, if he plays quartets with you?" When Schmidt heard me, however, he profoundly changed his prejudiced opinion and silently, a bond started to grow between us to which Schmidt remained faithful until the end.

'I must admit that in my whole life there was only one man with whom I had as profound a friendship as with Franz Schmidt. That was in my youth, and the man was Schoenberg: at the time, we made our first steps into the field of chamber music. Our enthusiasm was great and powerful. Schoenberg didn't have much of an idea of how to play the cello: he was a total autodidact. Nevertheless, despite his defective technique, a similar spiritual power radiated from his playing as, later, from Schmidt's.

'I take this opportunity to say a few words about the relation between the two masters: there was many a conversation in which Schmidt clearly expressed his opinion. He

Adler does not mention (although he is unlikely to have been unaware) that Schmidt tried to obtain for Schoenberg – as for Schreker – a teaching post at the Vienna Academy of Music but met with ministerial obstruction (the Academy had been taken over by the state in 1910). As a gesture for Schoenberg Schmidt organised the performance of *Pierrot lunaire* with his pupils on 15 April 1929; it met with high critical acclaim. The singer was Hilda Kretschmayr and the other performers were Walter Fidelsberger, Kurt Fuchsgelb, Hans Lewitus, Bruno Seidlhofer (the teacher of, *inter alios*, Jörg Demus, Friedrich Gulda and Paul Badura-Skoda) and Kamillo Wanausek. Schmidt is second from the left in the back row.

admired Schoenberg's gift for instrumentation and his talent as a tone-painter, as it first emerged in the *Gurrelieder* and the string sextet, *Transfigured Night*, in whose premiere by the Rosé Quartet Schmidt played the second cello, next to Buxbaum. When Schmidt himself was once asked where he had learnt his unfailing instrumentations, he replied: "From the same teacher from whom fish learn swimming". Schmidt was

extremely modest – as all great minds are. A little anecdote
may serve as evidence. When he wanted to attend a performance of Schoenberg's *Pierrot lunaire* in the Schoenberg Society,[2]
he patiently waited outside the door, until Schoenberg discovered him and led him into the hall. At a later stage, I shall
have to say more about his modesty. Never did his demeanour
evince the remotest trace of pride. On the aforementioned
occasion, he was quite overcome by *Pierrot*, which was conducted by Erwin Stein. What he unreservedly admired was
what he called Schoenberg's "wide ear", which went far
beyond the borders of accepted harmony.

'Deeply impressed by the work, he rehearsed it with his
students at the Academy and, before the performance, invited
Stein to listen to what he had achieved; after all, Stein
precisely knew the tradition of the work and Schmidt wanted
an expert's opinion: Stein didn't raise a single objection. This
is additional evidence of Schmidt's modesty.

'What I myself intensely admired in Schmidt was his
unfailing ear. Until this very day, I remember the principal
points of his speech when he became Rector – points about the
nature of the musical ear. *Inter alia*, his incomparable ear
showed whenever he reminded one of a theme by singing it: he
invariably sang it in its original key. There is deeper evidence
of his ear: he would, from memory, play any quartet or any
orchestral work on the piano, note-perfect and with all inner
parts.

'When Schmidt changed his prejudiced opinion about my
playing, he remarked to me: "You ask an awful lot of your
partners!" I felt it was from this moment that he saw in me the
violinist he had always wanted to have as a partner. And
indeed, it was from that moment that we met every week at
Mrs Saphir's, in order to play piano trios – almost the entire
classical literature. Under his hands, the piano underwent a
metamorphosis into another instrument: it became an adequ-
ate, organic means of expression for both the music of the

---

[2] Schoenberg's 'Society for Private Musical Performances', in which he
promoted performances of important contemporary works, the 'private'
referring to the fact that critics were not admitted: 'Kritikern ist der Eintritt
verboten'. –HK

masters and the spiritual quality of Schmidt's own musicality. His unfailing technique had nothing to do with digital dexterity: it was born out of his spiritual understanding of the music.'

After the relationship between Schmidt and Adler had grown into a 'true friendship', they naturally started to play string quartets together.

'The string quartet evenings took place every week in my flat in the Neubaugasse. "Here," said Schmidt, "is the real university for chamber music." The viola player was Dr Strassberg, perhaps Vienna's best viola player [not perhaps. – HK], while the second fiddler was the ultra-musical Elsy Stein, whose absolute assurance on her instrument could be described as somnambulistic; in her own musical life, she alternated between violin and viola. But reasons which I do not wish to mention led me a little later to change the ensemble into a men's quartet; I followed Wunderer's[3] advice: never take a woman into your quartet; it doesn't do any good. Accordingly, the second violin post was occupied by Brandmann or Fuchsgelb, both pupils of Schmidt's.[4] These quartet evenings turned into what can only be described as religious services. We played in my surgery; the faithful listeners were next door in the waiting room. Usually, the ritual began with two Haydn quartets, which were followed by Beethoven,[5] Brahms, Schumann, and Mendelssohn. Mendelssohn Schmidt loved above all other Romantics. Whenever we played a Mendelssohn quartet or quintet, he used to say, "and that's more than a hundred years old!"

'Two musicians spring to mind who occasionally played with us, although Schmidt couldn't stand them. One was the viola player of the Busch Quartet [Karl Doktor –HK], the

---

[3] Alexander Wunderer (1877–1955) was an oboist in the Vienna Philharmonic Orchestra and a friend of Schmidt. –HK

[4] And both later members of the then Palestine Philharmonic Orchestra, founded and auditioned by Toscanini and Huberman. –HK

[5] Adler forgot to list Mozart, a more frequent component than Brahms. – HK

other Hoffmann, a highly respected teacher at the Salzburg Mozarteum. With his fine nose, Schmidt immediately recognized Hoffmann as a future Nazi. Those two musicians reacted very much against our improvisatory style, which kept every work, however often we played it, as fresh and new as it felt when we first played it.

'Amongst the regular listeners I name only a few: Dr Erwin Ratz[6] . . ., Dr Josef Polnauer,[7] Olga Novakovic,[8] Mrs Grete Keller,[9] and her son Hans Keller, who already[10] has made an excellent name for himself as a writer on music . . . [Adler's further list comprises members of the Vienna Philharmonic and Schmidt pupils].

'Schmidt had a certain weakness for the female sex, which, however, never went too far. He was certainly flattered by all the crushes which many girls and women had on him, but he could become very angry when feminine pupils arrogated critical remarks to themselves and thus failed to show the necessary respect.
    . . .

'I now wish to discuss two essential points, to wit, his illness, and what seemed an unfortunate readiness to be influenced by extra-musical things, which included politics.

'Schmidt was already seriously ill when I got to know him, but he didn't know about his illness. In his youth he had been a passionate tea drinker, which circumstance may have led to a type of *diabetes insipidus*; also, he loved beer and schnaps a little too much. These loves were to show unfortunate consequences, i.e. cirrhosis of the liver, diabetes, and a deformation of the heart muscle. In addition, he suffered from hypertrophy of the prostate, which led to septic complications accompanied by high fever. He used to recover from these attacks and, for a short time, I was the doctor who treated

[6] An outstanding analyst whose writings should be translated as soon as at all possible. –HK
[7] A profound Schoenbergian analyst. –HK
[8] An outstanding pianist. –HK
[9] My mother. –HK
[10] Adler is writing in the Spring of 1954. –HK

him. One night, however, there was an ominous retention of urine, which eventually necessitated a bladder puncture. While this was a marvellous relief, the eventual operation was inescapable. However, a few days after his discharge from hospital, a septic infection again occurred; it lasted a very long time. A number of blood transfusions were eventually successful. Prior to the last transfusion, he asked me, "Do you still believe that I'll survive?" I replied with an emphatic "Yes!" In those days, I spent most of my time at his bedside, and we talked a lot. On one occasion, we came to talk about the Freemasons. A long time ago, Armin Saphir had persuaded him to join this order – but upon the advice of other friends, he left it again. He now seemed worried about leaving the order; he thought that this act might have been responsible for the deterioration of his health. We spent a long time over this subject, remembering and reminding each other of cases we had known. Fellow masons visited him and urged him to rejoin, but he remained adamant. Eventually, he could again be discharged from hospital, but he remained very weak, gaining weight at the same time; I dared not let him play quartets. On the last occasion we played in his house, in order to rehearse the Piano Quintet which he had written in response to a commission. If I am not mistaken, that was on 24 February 1938.

'During this time he composed his last and greatest work, the Oratorio, *The Book with Seven Seals*. One fact I have to state with all the emphasis at my disposal: Schmidt never was a Nazi. But politically, he was quite extraordinarily naive. In 1933, immediately after the burning of the Reichstag, we had our usual quartet evening, and I said: "Every child knows that this was a plot." "Let's go and play," he said evasively, and that's what we did. I further testify that on no occasion did Schmidt evince an anti-Semitic attitude. In fact, he once said, "Come to think of it, one can only mix with Jews". What he meant was, of course, spiritual Jews.

'An amusing episode occurs to me in this connection. At one time, a group of nationalistic German students turned to Schmidt with the request for a recommendation of a work by a contemporary composer which they could perform in their

circle.[11] What did he recommend? *Variations on a Hebrew Theme*
by Israel Brandmann, one of his composition pupils. His
spiritual outlook was not at all clerical; he was as deeply
religious as were all great masters. In his operas, the problem
of secularity *versus* mystical Christianity seems to have been
the basic subject, with the result that I often told him he must
have been a monk in a previous life, perhaps one of those
Swiss brothers who contributed greatly to the development of
polyphonic music.

'I would like to say a few words about his relation to
Mahler, and thereafter to Buxbaum.[12] As a conductor and
interpreter, Mahler commanded his unreserved respect, while
Mahler himself immediately recognized the genius of the
youthful Schmidt, who had to play all the solos, despite
Buxbaum's position as the principal cellist. I don't want to tell
tales, but the fact that Buxbaum felt he had been put into
second place can easily be understood, and his secret dislike of
Schmidt could be gleaned from occasional remarks he made.
Though Schmidt admired Mahler as a conductor, he did not
admire him as a composer. On one occasion he even described
Mahler's symphonies as "cheap novels". Such responses one
shouldn't really report. In his judgments, Schmidt wavered a
great deal, and very often contradicted himself. But a master
is always right, even if today he says the opposite of what he
said yesterday. Such judgments as the one I have quoted are
very often due to the mood of the moment. Schmidt became
very angry when other people criticized Mahler; he was
downright furious when Mahler's view of tradition, expressed
during an orchestral rehearsal, was thus misquoted: "Tradition is slovenliness".

'His greatest triumph was the first performance of the
oratorio. Unfortunately, I could not attend it, for I would
have been beaten up. The fact that the Nazis claimed him as
one of them and feted him in this sense wasn't his fault. But

[11] It must have been a political circle, for the 'nationalistic Germans'
(*Deutschnationalen*) were a political party, forerunners of the Nazis. –HK
[12] See p. 8 and Schmidt's comments in his *Autobiographical Sketch*, pp. 176–
179. –HK

the reasons for the BBC's negative attitude might perhaps be traced back to these events. Politically, he remained utterly naive. When I saw him for the last time, in order to take leave of him immediately prior to my departure for London, he asked me: "Why are you leaving, for heaven's sake?" He knew nothing of the horrors, nothing of the atrocities, nothing of Theresienstadt,[13] amongst whose victims was his viola player, Dr Strassberg, who was killed there. . . .

'He died at his desk, composing.'[14]

[13] A concentration camp. My grandmother was killed there – in her nineties. –HK

[14] This part of Adler's report has been contested. According to the administration of the Franz Schmidt Haus in Perchtoldsdorf, Schmidt died during lunch. His death was unexpected, despite his long history of illness. His sister Emma is said to have discovered him sitting upright in his chair. (His wife was on a shopping expedition in town.) –HK

To my wife,
who had to put up with me

INTRODUCTION

This book was written to commemorate Schmidt's 110th birthday.

I have shown in the course of the analyses that follow how I came to Franz Schmidt's music, and I think I have made it abundantly clear that I regard him as a very important composer. My reasons are many, but not the least is that for me the symphonic thinker is the ideal composer. I do not mean by this that all symphonists are great or supreme; there have been many poor symphonies, but there have been an astonishing number of very good ones, too. Of great symphonies the number is smaller, but there are more than one might think. And by symphonic thinker I do not only mean one who writes symphonies. I include the string quartet, the piano sonata, and works for various other combinations which have the quality of thought which I call symphonic. Inevitably, although not invariably, this involves sonata style, for me perhaps still the richest and most generous of modes of musical thought in what it has to yield. This, I know, is not at present a fashionable view. But I am not, and have no wish to be, a fashionable musician. And this, after all, is only *my* belief. No one is obliged to agree with it, and I shall be surprised (but nonetheless pleased) if anyone does. Study of Schmidt's Symphonies over a period of nearly fifty years has led me to the belief that he is one of the great symphonic thinkers, and that his achievements in this line are far-reaching and, so far as one can judge this at all, have lasting quality. They have the mark of genius in that the more one listens to them the more they reveal, both in thought and structure – the two are really indivisible.

There are other aspects of Schmidt's music which have led me to the conclusion that he was a great composer and one whose works should be known and studied as is the work of the older masters. Not the least are his unique lyrical and harmonic qualities. The lyricism requires no proof; one has only to listen to any Schmidt movement to hear it unmistakably. In fact, as I have shown, at times it came near presenting him with the kind of problem in symphonic structure that faced Schubert and Schumann. But, as they did, he solved the problem and avoided the pitfalls. His harmony is a mixture of tradition and twentieth century. Much of his thought is close to being what is mistakenly called bitonal: the E flat Prelude from the *Vier Kleine Präludien und Fugen* for organ is one very clear example. Much of his harmony is highly chromatic (in this lies his one visual, though not aural, relationship to Reger) and, in various but different ways, chromaticism is not only a nineteenth-century but also a twentieth-century feature. Schmidt's is definitely twentieth-century – although its prominence is astonishing in a composer who was himself colour-blind. There are certain types of chromatic usage, highlighted in the discussion of the symphonies that follows, by which one would know him instantly. But this is not the whole of it. Against this we may set a piece such as the *Weihnachtspräludium* for organ. This is harmonically plain throughout; he has eschewed any of the more usual complex harmony and the chromaticism which are the mark of so much of his organ writing, and has produced a piece which no less bears his mark – his, and no other's. Leaving aside the fact that it is one of the most deeply beautiful pieces of musical contemplation I have ever experienced, I do not profess to be able to put my finger on what does this. There is nothing obvious to give away the secret of the music, but the point is unmistakable. Schmidt has put his mark on this music as clearly and definitely as Beethoven put his on the bass at the beginning of the *Eroica* Variations.

And lastly, behind all Schmidt's work there is a deep sincerity, without pomposity.

ACKNOWLEDGEMENTS

Help in the production of this book has come from a variety of sources, not least the administration of the Franz Schmidt Haus in Perchtoldsdorf, the source of all the pictures and no little advice. Andrew Vores was meticulous in his copying of the music examples. Linda Ronaldson provided help with typing, and David Brown, Guy Rickards and Michael George found their offers of proof-reading eagerly accepted. Alan Soper, of the Central Music Library, London, deserves gratitude for help with the compilation of the Bibliography; and I am obliged to Messrs Glover and Blair for the quotations from Norbert Tschulik's *Franz Schmidt – A Critical Biography*.

HAROLD TRUSCOTT

I. BEGINNINGS

Franz Schmidt was born on 22 December 1874, in Pressburg, or Pozsony, which is now Bratislava and was also the birthplace of Hummel. Schmidt's *Autobiographical Sketch*[1] tells the story of his youth and early adulthood at rather more length, so I shall summarise briefly here. His father was of mixed German and Hungarian blood, his mother Hungarian. Both were musical and his mother gave Franz his first piano lessons. These were followed by tuition from a schoolteacher, Rudolf Mader, and Ludwig Burger, formerly a local theatre conductor. Neither of these seems to have made much of an impression. At thirteen Schmidt came under the influence of Helene von Bednarics, an art-lover who gathered friends, particularly those of artistic promise, about her in her house. Here Schmidt heard and was impressed by a considerable amount of music, but was repelled, even at his young age, by the fact that Fräulein von Bednarics, although she 'could hardly play', taught the piano.

Schmidt was later to have what has been called a love-hate relationship with the piano. We have the testimony of Josef Marx[2] and Hans Keller,[3] among others, as to his brilliance and perfect musicianship as a pianist, but he disliked a good deal of what he heard that passed for piano-playing, and even said on more than one occasion that the piano ruins the musical ear. This he repeated in a sort of essay, *Pianist or*

---

[1] *Autobiographische Skizze*, first published in part (with neither the knowledge nor permission of the copyright-holder, and in contradiction of Schmidt's express wish that his memoirs not appear until fifty years after his death) in Carl Nemeth, *Franz Schmidt: Ein Meister nach Brahms und Bruckner*, Amalthea Verlag, Zurich, 1957; it appeared in full in Otto Brusatti (ed.), *Studien zu Franz Schmidt*, Universal Edition for the Franz Schmidt Gemeinde, Vienna, 1976. It is published for the first time in English as an Appendix on pp. 156–182, Schmidt's 'embargo' having been broken for a long time now.

[2] *Wiener Zeitung*, 29 November 1953.

[3] See above, p. 7.

Musician?, which he put together in 1920.[4] In one place in this essay he delights my heart by stressing listening as the most important musical activity (apart, presumably, from the provision of the music), and especially what I may call the innocent ear – that of people who are deeply responsive to music but are not trained, professional musicians. His own attitude to piano-playing, as described by the pianist Friedrich Wührer,[5] Alfred Jirasek (Schmidt's brother-in-law),[6] and others, is sufficient proof of his right attitude to the instrument.

Fräulein von Bednarics suggested to Schmidt the famous piano-teacher, Theodor Leschetizky, and here 'pianist *or* musician' enters again, for it was Leschetizky who told his pupil, Artur Schnabel, that he would never be a pianist for he was a musician. That remark might have done damage, but fortunately did not, although one remark made by Leschetizky did. The harm that great men have done by ill-advised and supposedly witty remarks (the ephemeral wit obviously more important than the student) is incalculable. After Schmidt had triumphantly played Liszt and Balakirev's *Islamey* to much applause, Leschetizky said: 'There's potential there, even quite a lot! But the fellow will never be tidy. Anyway, someone with a name like Schmidt shouldn't become an artist'. Schmidt summed up his reaction in one sentence: 'I never wanted to touch another piano again'.[7] That was in 1888 when he was fourteen, but the sting of Leschetizky's 'witticism' stayed with him and coloured much of his thought.

Schmidt did touch the piano again, beautifully, but Leschetizky's careless remark may have much to do with the fact that among Schmidt's mature music what little there is for piano, with the exception of two small pieces, is with other instruments and is the result of commissions from Paul Wittgen-

---

[4] An English translation appears as an Appendix to Volume II of this study.

[5] Quoted in Norbert Tschulik, *Franz Schmidt – A Critical Biography*, Glover & Blair, London, 1980, p. 33 (Österreichischer Bundesverlag, Vienna, 1972).

[6] *ibid.*, p. 34.

[7] See *Autobiographical Sketch*, p. 165–166.

stein, the pianist who lost his right arm in the 1914–18 War
and thereafter made a career as a pianist playing with his left
hand. Thus nearly all of Schmidt's mature piano music is for
left hand only. One unguarded moment of misguided wit has
debarred us from possessing a really fruitful body of solo
music for an instrument Schmidt played and understood so
well.

While Schmidt's future with the piano was being thus
kicked about, his other musical studies seem to have been
neglected, except for what he could glean for himself. Before
he went into Bruckner's counterpoint class at the Conservatoire of the Gesellschaft der Musikfreunde in 1890 (which was
abortive, since Bruckner had leave of absence for illness from
which he never returned), the only instruction he had seems to
have come from a Franciscan monk, Felician Josef Moczik
(1861–1917). Moczik was a painter, not a musician, although
he did play the organ; but he was not a pianist, and so he
simply listened for hours to Schmidt's playing. In his autobiography, which goes up to the year 1914, the composer
writes that the Franciscan had 'the deepest and most enduring
influence on my entire development as human being and
artist'.

Schmidt's first preserved efforts at composition do not go
far to bear this out, although it may, of course, be a case of
delayed effect. In 1889 he began to write the first of two piano
sonatas; both were completed in 1890 when Schmidt was
fifteen. 'Piano sonatas' is a courtesy title, for both works show
quite unequivocally that, whatever intellectual notion he may
have had of what constituted a piano sonata, in practical
composition he had no idea at all. Despite his prowess as a
pianist, the two works suggest nothing so much as a crude
transcription for piano of an equally crude attempt at orchestral writing. In addition to the absence of a real technique of
piano writing, they lack ideas and a real sense of composition,
including that of movement. Even Wagner in 1831 did better
than Schmidt in 1889 (true, he was a few years older then than
Schmidt was but he had far less musical experience).

At about the same time Schmidt produced a work for piano
duet, *Schellen-Einzugsmarsch*, but I do not know this (it is

The official photograph of Schmidt as Rector of the Academy of Music and the Performing Arts in Vienna.

currently lost) and cannot comment. Also, since Schmidt describes the second of the two Sonatas as Op. 7, clearly there were earlier compositional attempts which have not survived. Schmidt said that he 'would painstakingly destroy everything which remained a draft, did not turn out well, or did not satisfy him'.[8] These two works were saved by his two sisters, despite his intentions, and thus escaped his vigilance; personally, I am glad they did, for they supply a very interesting glimpse of where he started as a composer, although they do nothing to enhance his reputation. Thus there is little if anything to explain the enormous leap forward from 1889–90 with these two 'sonatas' to 1896 with the beginning of his First Symphony.

Schmidt's slow development as a composer is partly bound up with the family's failing fortune. His father, who had been an officer in the Imperial Army before entering the removals business, was unaccountably involved in an attempted fraud and was given a reduced prison sentence. This brought with it the end of the family business, his mother's straitened means, which she augmented to some extent by sewing, and work for Franz. When his father was released he managed to get a job as a book-keeper, and his son 'gave lessons, rehearsed opera singers, taught mathematics, and used his knowledge of Hungarian as a translator'.[9] All this, plus the disgrace of his father's attempted fraud and imprisonment, which he felt keenly, acted as a partial drag on Schmidt's musical progress. Furthermore, he was naturally a slow developer (up to a point) and these circumstances, coupled with his self-criticism, probably explain the dearth of surviving compositions between 1890 and 1896.

Bruckner's lessons being non-existent, Schmidt began to study with Robert Fuchs, a much-respected teacher and composer of some outstanding piano sonatas and other piano music, and chamber music (he was known in Vienna as 'Serenaden-Fuchs' because of his contributions to that genre, which was then very popular in the Austrian capital). Yet

[8] Tschulik, *op. cit.*, p. 16.
[9] *ibid.*, p. 16; *cf.* the *Autobiographical Sketch*, p. 173.

Schmidt was not happy in his lessons and preferred to work on his own (if one is capable of it, there is no better way to learn). However, he did have cello lessons at the Academy (where he stored his cello with the porter) with Ferdinand Hellmesberger, who judged him, wrongly, as 'not exactly talented, but really very diligent' – but Schmidt scarcely ever practised, and yet he could produce fine playing and a superb tone to order.

During this period at the Academy Schmidt wrote four *Fantasiestücke nach Ungarischen Nationalmelodien* for cello and piano. The first Schmidt suppressed because it was very similar to the second (the first of the published three). The remaining three were published, like a good deal of Schmidt's music, much later – in 1926, just thirty-four years after they were written. They have a good deal more to offer than the two Sonatas in ideas and general construction, but for the piano very little more. What there is is pianistic, which is a gain, but the piano parts are purely accompaniment, and of the simplest kind – chordal support to a rhapsodic cello part. In the latter there are tiny sporadic glimpses of the Hungarian voice that shot out suddenly fully formed in the orchestral *Intermezzo* he wrote in 1902–3 and which was absorbed into his first opera, *Notre Dame*.

In 1896 Schmidt drew praise from Brahms for a cadenza to a Haydn cello concerto. He graduated from the Academy with distinction and, also in 1896, obtained a post as cellist in the Vienna Court Opera Orchestra, which automatically made him a member of the Vienna Philharmonic Orchestra. Later, from 1901, he taught the cello at the Conservatoire.

Schmidt's thoughts were turning towards opera – a curious choice, it seems to me, for a mind more attuned to the symphony and chamber music I cannot imagine. But although opera engaged him, and a few years later he produced *Notre Dame*, his first bow as a major composer was, appropriately, as a symphonist.

28

II. SYMPHONY NO. 1 IN E MAJOR
(1896–99)

Taking the other three Symphonies, and especially the Third and Fourth, as accurate indications of the nature of a Schmidt symphony, the First is only partly a true example of his symphonic art. Except for what the music tells us, it is difficult to know what was going through his mind when he wrote it. Despite the thoughts of opera which would coalesce into *Notre Dame*, the First Symphony is quite different from the opera, as it is from the three later Symphonies and most of his other music. It is not less important, for it contains the key to most of what came later, but it stands apart, rather as most of the organ music, his second opera, *Fredigundis*, and the oratorio, *Das Buch mit Sieben Siegeln*, are apart, each in a different way. The Symphony, which won a prize given by the Gesellschaft der Musikfreunde of Vienna, was first performed on 25 January 1902 by the Konzertvereinsorchester, conducted by the composer.

Much of its music does not make anything like its full impact until we realise that the spiritual home of the first and last movements is the late Baroque. The real composer of these two movements is a Handel fitted out with a late-nineteenth-century technique, adapting his ideas and the new technique to the service of the symphony he never knew. The two movements recognise and use the language of the Baroque as it suits them, which, as part of a mixture involving nineteenth-century style, is almost unique. And as part of a large-scale symphony, it is quite unique. But the late Baroque began to affect composers quite early in the nineteenth century. No later than 1825 Mendelssohn (in whom Schmidt had an abiding interest) produced his *Seven Characteristic Pieces*, Op. 7, for piano, which already reflect his lifelong interest in Handel by including an *allemande*, *sarabande* and a fugue, separated by other pieces of a purely nineteenth-century cut; but these made no impact in bringing the Baroque to the fore.

A little later Mendelssohn was instrumental in bringing Bach back to public attention, the effects of which were widespread, especially in such composers as Schumann and Brahms, and many more.

One of the profoundest results, complete and on a considerable scale, came from Adolf Jensen (1837–79), usually regarded as a minor composer, but who was in fact no mean master. He wrote, among other things, one of the greatest piano sonatas of the century, in F sharp minor, Op. 25, a work which pianists would do well to consider, and some wonderful songs, among which are some settings from the *Spanish Song Book* which predate Hugo Wolf's and are equally fine, although differently conceived. Also to his credit is the work I am concerned with here, the *Deutsche Suite*, Op. 36. In spite of its title, it is what was known as a French suite. Beginning with an *allemande*, it is superbly conceived and carried out, utilising all the suggestion of the seventeenth-century suite combined with nineteenth-century harmony and piano keyboard mastery. It is no harpsichord work but one fully conceived for the piano, with Jensen's own nineteenth-century ideas imbued with the spirit of the French suite – a genuine case of an old bottle yielding quite new contents – and since Jensen's music in this work could scarcely have been expressed in any other way, it is a real artistic landmark. It was composed during the 1860s, under what spur of inspiration I do not know, except for Jensen's stroke of genius in uniting style and content. Thus it appeared some years before Schmidt was born, and it is possible that he encountered it. Whether he did or not, it helped to put a certain spirit abroad in German music. (There were at least two subsequent piano works, each individual to its composer and among their finest (and least known) productions. The first of these was the *Suite* in D minor by Eugen d'Albert, published as his Op. 1, where, in the *allemande* especially, he seems to have been moved by his knowledge of the Jensen work. The other one is the latest, the *Suite in the Olden Style*, Op. 24, by Ernst von Dohnányi, composed in 1913. All three make the *sarabande* the deepest and most moving part of the suite. Not one contains a fugue, but there is plenty of fine, fluent counterpoint, and all three among the works I most enjoy playing.¹)

The spirit which Jensen infused into German nineteenth-century music with his suite eventually spread, I believe, into the twentieth century with its re-awakened interest in Baroque music. (Reger, of course, is the composer most often cited as having roots in the Baroque past, and yet, strangely, not one of the works to which he gave the title 'suite' is in any sense a Baroque suite.) And this is where Schmidt's First Symphony comes in. Whatever the cause, something blew a gust of the Baroque in his direction in time for it to affect the E major Symphony.

The finale was written first, at quite some distance from the rest of the work, so that it may or may not have been originally designed as part of the Symphony. It may even have been written, as Tschulik suggests,² as an exercise. If so, it is remarkable both for its size and for the fact that it carries no such character with it. Whether by accident or design, what it does suggest, from the very first bar, is exactly what it was eventually used for – the finale of a large-scale work. It could not possibly be the beginning of anything, without bad miscalculation on the part of the composer or doing damage to what might follow.

First Movement: Sehr Langsam – Sehr Lebhaft

The immediate overall impression of the first movement is that the movement is quite short for such a large-scale late-nineteenth-century symphony, even that its end comes unexpectedly soon. The second impression is that the orchestra (apart from a double-bassoon, a third trumpet and a bass tuba, each very sparingly used) is of Classical size and is used for the most part with Classical restraint. There are three trombones, but Schubert had used these, and Brahms had

---

¹ Although d'Albert had a French father and was born in Glasgow, he had allied himself completely with German music. Dohnányi, although Hungarian (he, too, was born – as Ernö Dohnányi – in Pozsony, three years after Schmidt), here used a German idiom which he made his own.

² *op. cit.*, p. 20.

Ex. 1

used the double-bassoon. The work begins with an introduction, and immediately (Ex. 1) we are confronted with one of the Baroque elements, for it sounds like the large beginning of a French overture, if with a scale of tone no Baroque composer ever dreamed of. Note the rising horn figures; they are important. The dotted rhythm gives place to a lyrical and evenly paced cadence theme for woodwind, horns and violins, and this leads to a quiet rising trumpet theme, also cadential, which moves without a break into the main movement, *Sehr Lebhaft (Allegro)*. This sets off (Ex. 2a) with a four-horn fanfare

Ex. 2

developing the rising horn figures of Ex. 1. A *tutti* (Ex. 2b) turns this by variation into a four-square theme using the dotted rhythm we have already heard at the outset, but at a smart pace and with a distinctly classical character.

Two particularly foolish conclusions have in the past been drawn from the music I have so far described. One[3] is that the

---

[3] Kurt Honolka, quoted in Tschulik, *op. cit.*, pp. 9 and 20.

work was influenced by Bruckner's Seventh Symphony, on two counts: firstly, the rising trumpet theme and the horn fanfare, for Bruckner's Seventh begins with a theme on cello and horn in unison, far longer than either of the Schmidt themes, and the Bruckner theme also rises up the chord of E major. That the two, Bruckner's theme and Schmidt's two ideas, have no connection in sound or character obviously was not considered, if it was even noticed. (When musicologists are on this sort of track they see only what they want to see.) The other count was the fact that Schmidt's Symphony is in E major, as is Bruckner's. E major is certainly a rare key for a symphony; off-hand I can think of six others: Haydn's No. 12, Schubert's Seventh, which was genuinely unfinished,[4] Raff's Fifth (*Lenore*), Glazunov's First, the Fourth Symphony by the great Swiss symphonist, Fritz Brun, and Dohnányi's Second Symphony. But keys are open for anyone's use; no composer has proprietary rights in them. In this instance there is no connection between Schmidt's music and Bruckner's other than key (and initial scoring). Tonal composers, in any case, tend more often than not to write their music in the key in which they first hear it mentally, unless there is any technical reason for altering it.

The other criticism[5] is that part of Schmidt's *Allegro* theme, the *tutti* version, Ex. 2b, resembles the opening theme of Strauss's *Don Juan* and to an extent it does, although it is not the same, and plays a totally different part in the whole. One immediate difference is that Schmidt's *tutti* theme has a classical sound, and nothing could make Strauss's *Don Juan* theme sound classical. (One further 'connection' has apparently escaped the critics: the first violin figure in the fourth bar of Schmidt's *tutti* theme, Ex. 2b, is, so far as it goes, the same as one bit of the 'big' theme in Strauss's tone-poem, *Tod und Verklärung* (fig. a).)

[4] The English musicologist Brian Newbould has recently – and very speculatively – done the job for him; and there are two previous completions, by John Barnett and by Felix Weingartner. My preference is for Weingartner's.

[5] Tschulik, *op. cit.*, p. 20. He says 'second subject' although he means the second theme to be heard (his terminology is loose and vague throughout).

The *tutti* passage expands, lands on the dominant and continues from there, expands still further on matter drawn from that fourth bar of Ex. 2, and closes back on to the tonic. So far the music has been consistently built on the common chord figure which started the introduction, through the trumpet theme, the horn fanfare and the *tutti*, and the material has passed, in character, from Baroque to Classical. It now moves a stage further on, as Schmidt begins the balancing act he manages so superbly in this movement. Not only is the music that follows now in striking contrast to what has preceded it, in that it is quiet, lyrical and flowing, but it is distinctly late-nineteenth-century in character.

Although expansions have occurred twice in the music immediately before this point, they are small and the overall feeling of the music so far, including the brief introduction, is rather one of contraction, almost as though it were being compressed into a container too small for it. With the passage we have now reached the music suddenly relaxes, as if released from constriction. Purists might feel that the mixture of styles and the sudden passing from restriction to the lyrical expansion we have now reached could constitute a fault in the construction of the music. The danger is there; I believe that Schmidt has avoided it. His fusion of mixed elements, Baroque, Classical, Romantic, as well as the time-scale of each, is handled with a confident mastery which, as one recalls what of his earlier efforts at composition we know, is nothing short of marvellous. It is not so much the size of the work as it is this completely confident handling of diverse and almost contra-dictory elements that I had in mind when I wrote of the enormous leap forward from 1889–90 to 1896, for the three *Fantasiestücke* of 1892 add nothing in way of explanation.

One of the reasons for the success of a rather dangerous scheme lies in a feature (Ex. 4) we now encounter on our way to the second group. It is possible that the three crotchets that begin this new lyrical tune grow from that fourth bar of Ex. 2 or Ex. 2, fig. a; it is possible that they came the other way about, as it is also possible that there was no conscious connection between them in the composer's mind but simply that he tended to think in a way he had already thought in this

movement. The one could have unconsciously affected the
other; where such connections do appear they are more often
than not unconscious connections on the composer's part. So
much that happens creatively is the result of the composer's
mind already having been steered or having steered itself
along a certain path. Here is the beginning of the new theme,
Ex. 3a, and part of its continuation a few bars later, Ex. 3b.
Ex. 4 follows it almost immediately.

Ex. 3

Ex. 4

So far, with one exception, and including the introduction,
where one would not in so short a space expect any deviation,
the phrasing has been regular, four-bar phrases or multiples of
four. The exception comes with the arrival of Ex. 2, where
what easily could have been eight bars is extended to ten.
With Ex. 3 the phrasing is still of four bars, followed by
another extension, this time to six bars. In spite of the two
extensions nothing has so far interfered with the even flow of
four beats to the bar. Now something does. We have already
in the follow-up to Ex. 3 a suggestion of new movement merely
by the chromatic alternation of harmonies: D major, followed
by F sharp, followed by G major, back to F sharp, each for
half a bar. And in bar 5 of this six-bar period occurs Ex. 4,
which is simply a thematic rhythm plucked from Ex. 3b. A bar
later the music moves on to a new figure (Ex. 5). I have shown
the woodwind movement as well as that of the strings, for

Ex. 5

together they make a fascinating sound. But quite as important here, after so much even movement of four beats to a
bar, is the introduction of a genuine cross-rhythm – three-
crotchet rhythm across the prevailing four-crotchet. The
music does not simply become three-four for the time being for
both three- and four-beat rhythms can be heard simultaneously – not an easy thing to bring off, when all the music seems,
in one way or another, to be stressing the beat of three. All is
repeated a fourth higher from Ex. 4, and the repetition leads
straight on to the beginning of the second group, in B major,
with what is, in this context, one of the most astonishing
passages in all Schmidt's music. But it needs all the context,
all the lead-in, to give it the sound and character it has (Ex.
6). Here is, at one and the same time, the apotheosis of Exx. 4
and 5, in this wonderful sound of three beats across four. Also,
the cross-rhythm is double, for the theme can be heard either
as a three-crotchet rhythm or as one of three minims. It is in
the nature of the music that it should be repeated, this time at
the same pitch, but with different scoring, and the final bar,
sliding back to an uncomplicated four beats, moves as
smoothly as though oiled. No jolt is felt, but four-beat rhythm
is back.

Ex. 6

It was an essential in the conveying of the character of this music that all this complex pattern of thought should be achieved as smoothly as a ride in a new Rolls-Royce. Indeed, if one were aware of jolts the entire thing would have failed. But the amount of imaginative technique that went into its making, so that the technique is not even suggested in the resulting sound, was phenomenal.

Consistent growth of thought is one of the deepest qualities of real symphonic thinking, of which Ex. 4 gives us an example, for its significance stretches back beyond its actual first appearance. When Ex. 2 moves on to the dominant, it gains the addition in Ex. 7. What I have marked as fig. a already heralds, with a different rhythm, the approach of Ex. 4, and I have already detailed its further history; it is also prominent in the climax that leads to Ex. 3.

Ex. 7

With the resumption of plain four-beat rhythm, the harmony hovering all round the dominant of B, it is again Ex. 4, following its rhythmic disruptive character, that resettles the music in a four-crotchet time. A derivative makes a four-bar introduction to the final part of the exposition, a new tune (Ex. 8) which also brings with it a slight increase of speed. This too is repeated, and sinks to rest on B, and in the last bars of the exposition clarinet, followed by a horn, state the theme of the horn fanfare, spread out over whole bars, which leads to the original fanfare and the repetition of the exposition.

Ex. 8

The second time around, the drawn-out fanfare leads on to
the development, where its relationship to Ex. 2a is made
clear enough by yet another version of the fanfare theme. Ex.
2b follows, still in E minor, the harmony moves out to G
major, and the climax that led to Ex. 3 ensues here and leads
again to Ex. 3. Four bars of this takes the music to E flat and a
momentary new fragment of tune (Ex. 9), related rhythmically
to Ex. 3.

Ex. 9

One of the most important aspects of this passage is the
continual flow of quavers in the manner of so much of the
exposition, and, towards the end of Ex. 9, the chromatic
alternation of harmonies already noted in the follow-up to Ex.
3; another is the chromatically descending harmony shown in
Ex. 3, a long-drawn-out version of Ex. 4. So many threads are
drawn together here. Bar 4 of Ex. 2 gains a new, enlarged
character and is succeeded by Ex. 4 on woodwind and horns,
punctuating Ex. 8 on violins. The process is repeated from the
last appearance of Ex. 3, Ex. 9 now coming on a swing to B
major, followed by Ex. 8, still punctuated by Ex. 4. At its
close, the drawn-out version of the horn fanfare theme, as at
the end of the exposition, arises in trumpet and horns, much
expanded this time.

At this point I think Schmidt made his only real mistake in
the Symphony. This drawn-out version of the fanfare has so
fine an effect, growing as it does out of what precedes it, and
already bringing about in a new way the conditions originally
achieved by the actual horn fanfare, that I feel it should lead
straight on to Ex. 2. Instead, Schmidt delays the arrival of
that *tutti* by inserting the original horn version of the fanfare,
which he has now made quite redundant. At a crucial moment
in the piece it impedes, holds back, the movement of the

music. It is his one failure of imagination in this work.

The recapitulation flows on, the counterstatement of Ex. 2 switched to the subdominant, A major. This brings the whole transition passage unchanged and the second group in E minor and major, joined on to a fairly large coda, which is based on the drawn-out version of the fanfare, with the persistent quaver movement and interjections from Ex. 4.

In this movement, which shows little or nothing in the way of influence, its ideas and processes of thought being already deeply tinged with an early type of Schmidtian character, there is one short passage, which comes a number of times, which just momentarily sounds like another composer. That composer is Carl Goldmark. Goldmark is usually written off as a minor composer, and wrongly so, for he had one of the most personal styles of writing I have come across. I would undertake to recognise him in a matter of a few bars from any work of his which I do not already know (which does not mean that he is always repeating himself any more than it does with Brahms or Sibelius): Goldmark sounds like no one else. And one of his most personal characteristics is his orchestration, which will easily betray him in any passage of reasonable length. (It was to Goldmark, incidentally, that Sibelius went in Vienna for lessons in orchestration, and it is perhaps not surprising that there are traces of Goldmark's impress in some of Sibelius's earlier work.) The passage in Schmidt's movement to which I refer occurs nine bars from the end of the exposition; it recurs a few times more, always with the same orchestral effect, which will be recognised by anyone who knows Goldmark's overture *Im Frühling*, where it occurs prominently. Its appearance in Schmidt's movement could be, and probably was, quite accidental, but its power to call up the other composer (also Hungarian) is undeniable, and worth noting in a movement singularly lacking in influences.

The high organisation of this comparatively short movement is due a great deal to the masterly handling of three different time-scales and sets of period elements. And this has its effect on what follows. There are three different kinds of pace in this movement: there is the Baroque type of the introduction, slow-moving and with little or no harmonic pace to disturb its centre; there is the classical pace of the first group; and that of the transition passage and second group, which is a combination of both the previous types. This moves with a rapidity equal to but different from that of the first group, in that it embodies the slow with the fast. As far as I know, Schubert was the first composer to do this; Schmidt's example, however, is characteristic of him, not of Schubert. Already at the beginning of the main movement the horn fanfare gives a faint taste of this dramatic slowness before it moves on to the pace of what follows. The manner in which the speed of the second group easily accommodates the drawn-out versions of that fanfare without disturbing their context is due to this dual nature in the pace of the music.

So there are two types of slow pace in this movement, one of them mingled with a real fast tempo. But now this first movement is succeeded by one in which stillness, absence of movement, is taken as far as it can be without the music quite ceasing to move. It is yet a different kind of slow pace – it is almost no pace at all. It lies at the heart of things, and barely a ripple moves out from its centre.

Second Movement: Langsam

Almost inaudibly Schmidt begins his slow movement. From a chord of E flat the music moves to the harmony of A flat minor and back, then to F flat major and back. This beginning is interesting, tonally and harmonically, and it has deceived at least one of Schmidt's critics. Tschulik writes that the movement 'begins in E flat major, but immediately moves into nuances of the minor'.[6] Whether or not this knowledge was gained aurally or visually, the E flat is, in fact, the dominant of A flat, and Schmidt has given the music the key-signature of four flats – that of A flat major. It is a gentle way into the key, from the E major of the first movement, both simple and subtle at the same time. The move down a semitone is simple

[6] *op. cit.*, p. 20.

enough (as simple as Brahms' gaining his E flat dominant by
a similar step after the B major trio in the middle movement of
his E flat Clarinet Sonata), but the flavour of the result of
Schmidt's device is subtle, almost elusive.

After his gentle introduction the main tune floats in on a
clarinet with a sigh, its gentleness enhanced by a touch of
mystery in the harmony (Ex. 10). In such surroundings the
simplest deviations carry with them a touch of the remote. A
sequential answer to Ex. 10 carries the music on to a more
fully scored repetition; then, with a sighing coda, on a new
little idea derived *in mood* from what precedes it, it eases its
way out on a long-drawn final chord.

Ex. 10

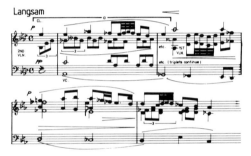

Schmidt, as I have said, gives this movement the four-flat
key-signature of A flat major, and this is the basic key of the
movement, as events prove. But so far the key is A flat *minor*;
throughout the tune the composer has written whatever extra
flats are needed where they are required. However, in spite of
the minor key the music is quietly, unexcitedly happy. But
now, with another of the simple magical shifts that are so
much in the blood of this music, a tune arises in E major. This
is genius, mastery, a share, in whatever degree, of the quality
Beethoven possessed in abundance, the ability to make the old
vividly new, as though it had never been heard before. In fact,
it is no more than the taking of the tonic, A flat, as the third of
a new basic chord, E major, a device almost as old as music,
certainly as old as classical music. But it sounds here like a
new discovery. This is the real creativity. In a chorus of four

Ex. 11

horns this tune sails gloriously above and around us. In Ex. 11 I give the first of its three phrases. They are separated by quiet woodwind interjections of a pastoral nature, of which I also give the first. The second phrase of the horn theme is the same length as the first, the third three times as long, with a beautiful climactic curve. As it finishes strings enter and, with slow demisemiquavers supported by triplets, with slower (or larger) chords on woodwind and brass, build up a crescendo and diminuendo on a chord of E major which covers three bars – at this tempo a huge distance. This leads to a beautifully re-scored and fuller-toned restatement of the horn tune, the interjections now given to the horns.

The final cadence is echoed and re-echoed, and from it Ex. 10 arises in E minor, and is built gradually to two climaxes, progressive in turbulence; one is built on the sequential answer phrase diminished in size, which lands on D flat minor, the second uses Ex. 10a. The scheme is simple, as simple as the harmonic devices I have already referred to; the still happiness of the first part of the movement must be tested, and the turbulence does this. For one critic, the notorious Eduard Hanslick, the turbulence represented Cossacks murdering and burning, and destroyed the movement. Well, that is one way of looking at it – and in this case 'looking' is the operative word;[7] a better way is to hear Schmidt's whole plan, and then the true inwardness of the opening music of this movement makes itself felt the more because of the orderly and restrained tumult that has intervened.

[7] I have sometimes thought that when Hanslick misguidedly turned his attention to music the world lost an inspired lavatory attendant.

The second climax arrives at a first inversion chord of C major, where trombones, *fff*, intone the beginning of Ex. 11, followed by trumpets on the same phrase. The peak of the climax is a descending cadenza passage on first violins, depending from the first two rising notes of Ex. 11, on the harmony of D flat minor. This brings Ex. 11 fully restated in A flat major, trumpets replacing the original horns, strings glowingly giving the original woodwind interjections. A short, quiet coda, based on fragments of Ex. 11 joined in one melodic line, brings the movement to its appointed end.

Third Movement: Schnell und Leicht

A Schmidt scherzo is something rare, to be savoured. I used to think that, in so far as the Bruckner-type scherzo had any successors, they were Schmidt's. There may be a small core of truth in this; but the more I listen to Bruckner's the more I realise that there is not just one type, and the more I listen to Schmidt's the more I realise how vastly different they are. Bruckner's could have been a spur, but they were certainly never anything more. But there is, in the scherzi in the first three Symphonies, as well as in some of the chamber works, a distinct echo of the Austrian *Ländler*; they are faster than that dance is as a rule, but the spirit is there, and it is never remotely present in any of Bruckner's scherzi. (Its influence *can* be heard in some of his trios, but not in the scherzi.)

Eight bars, establishing the persistent quaver motion of the movement, and starting from A flat turned to G sharp, lead to the beginning of the scherzo proper. It begins with a leap upward of a sixth, and it is upward leaps of an octave that lead to it (Ex. 12). The flavour of this music cannot be conveyed in words; only the music can do that. It is personal, yet there are none of the chromatic elements that make up so much of Schmidt's later language, until we reach the closing, more song-like, portion of the first part. Nonetheless, the music conveys a highly idiosyncratic sound. Even in that closing portion (Ex. 13) it is a good deal the lightly grinding bass F sharp against the upper moving harmonies that gives the

Ex. 12

Ex. 13

phrases their character, although only a minor ninth is involved.

Then there is the phrasing itself. For any composer writing sonata music who has so much of the naturally lyrical in his nature as Schmidt had, the handling of phrasing is of unusual importance. With a naturally dramatic gift, such as Beethoven's or Haydn's, this will, in a sense, take care of itself; but with such as Schmidt it has to be made to take care. (Schubert was an earlier master who had and solved the same problem.) And it is precisely in such a movement as this, where the lyrical in phrasing is natural to the music, that slight departures from the normal make themselves felt (again, as they did in Schubert). Just one or two such things are enough to stiffen the fabric and give it a character that will bend but not break.

There are two such instances in the present case, up to the end of the first part. Ex. 12b is the beginning of a normal eight-bar phrase; the counterstatement, with its somewhat different harmonic movement to take it to the dominant, reaches that harmony in nine bars. The extra bar flows in naturally, but immediately removes any feeling of squareness. Then Ex. 13 begins to move in four-bar phrases; we have two of them, followed by the beginning of a third, which turns out to be three bars, followed by four to close the first part of this scherzo. In fact, this extension is more subtle than the first one, for really that third phrase *is* of four bars, but the fourth bar is an overlap, acting also as the beginning of the final four-bar phrase.

From a rising B major quaver arpeggio the second part opens out with a downward leap of a sixth, switching the harmony to F sharp minor with a delicious answer. This fills eight bars and is followed by a sequence – the whole thing again down one tone. Again the extra ninth bar intervenes, the harmony now become G major, and the original closing phrases of Ex. 13 ensue, taking the harmony to E flat major and an abrupt stop in mid-air, after three bars of a normal four-bar phrase, succeeded by two silent bars. Then Ex. 12b is heard on E flat harmony, much slower and very tentatively, played by three flutes with a dominant horn pedal. It gets as far as the sixth bar, which is repeated, the music gathering momentum, and sweeps at full speed into a complete restatement in E major of Ex. 12b and the answer phrase only of Ex. 13, with a simple interval change to keep the music on the tonic. Thus the E flat statement serves the purpose of the original first eight-bar phrase, with a twist.

Once again comes the simple semitonal change from E flat harmony to the real key of E major, and again note its effectiveness. This is the end of the scherzo proper; it is a wonderful movement, simple as is all the most effective music. Its persistent pattering harmonic counterpoint, mainly on the strings, is as magical in its effect as its thematic ideas, and contributes a great deal to the overall impression of the piece.

What follows is something of a puzzle in a normal scherzo and trio. The effect is almost as though, having completed his scherzo, Schmidt thought of more he wanted to say in the same style – but not in the same mood. Tschulik's attitude to it, in sum, is to ignore it. He writes: 'A section which is to be played "slowly, but without dragging", taking the function of

a Trio, displays a Romantic sound-palette, entrusted above all
to the strings'.[8] That is all (our analysis has yet to come to the
'slow, but not dragging' episode); he betrays no consciousness
of anything unusual. Later[9] he quotes a review from the time
of the first performance, which speaks of 'the Scherzo, with its
two Trios'; this, while not yet accurate, at least shows
sufficient perspicacity to note something unusual, even if the
conclusion drawn does not go sufficiently deep. Even this does
not jolt Tschulik; he remains incurious. If the reviewer (Dr
Theodor Helm) is right, this is the strangest such movement
with two trios in my experience. At any rate, without a break
or even the slightest pause the scherzo, from its final bar,
plunges into C sharp minor and a mood which suggests that a
dark cloud has covered the sun which shone only a moment
before (Ex. 14). Technically, a diminished-seventh quaver

Ex. 14

arpeggio releases a theme which climbs almost throughout in
minor thirds, changing once to a major, once to an augmented
second. It can be seen that the quaver movement still
continues in second violins and cellos, while a descending bass
completes the main texture. The woodwind, however, is
riddled with imitations of the figure I have marked *a*, which is
a simple turn. With different scoring the phrase is repeated,
and the two phrases are directed to be repeated entire. The
second part has the upper theme of Ex. 14 in the bass, starting
from B, with quaver movement on top and sustained woodwind outlining the descending upper notes of the quaver line.
The rising bass moves through to the treble, quavers (not the
same ones) are transferred to the bass, and this is capped by a
new figure (Ex. 15), of shakes and chromatic semiquavers,
which hints at some of Schmidt's Hungarian feeling and,

[8] *op. cit.*, p. 20.
[9] *ibid.*, p. 22.

Ex. 15

much developed, is the kind of idea which features a lot in his later music. Everything from the rising bass version of Ex. 14 is repeated, followed by one statement of Ex. 14 at its original pitch, and this leads to a more tranquil passage with new and more lyrical development of the turn (fig. a, Ex. 14) the purpose of which is to calm down the music and lead to – well, in a normal, well-conducted scherzo with two trios it would lead to a repetition of the scherzo, as in the similar case in Beethoven's Seventh Symphony and other such cases in various works of Schumann. Here it does not, and this is the curious feature that Herr Tschulik should at least have glanced at, instead of ignoring it as if it were not there.

What the tranquil passage leads to is a slow $\frac{6}{8}$ piece in D flat major, the major version of C sharp minor, enharmonically written (this is the 'slow, but not dragging' section of which Tschulik wrote). The immediate connection is through a passage built on a theme of rising seconds, which are at last echoed by four muted horns, from which the strings, also muted, slide into D flat. But this is not a second trio: it is the other half, or the other side, of the one to which we have been listening. The whole trio is two-faced, like a coin, or like Janus. The characters are different, but the opposition of the two is similar. The D flat portion is not a reflection of the C sharp minor passage, but it is rather thrown off by it, and completes the sense. The cloud has moved on, not immediately revealing the scherzo; the picture is not yet the same as before. A new aspect is before us, gentle, rocking, almost floating.

The most important point about this music in Schmidt's work as a whole is that it is the closest, over quite a long stretch, too, that this Symphony comes to a prominent part of mature, characteristic Schmidt. It moves from D flat on to A

Schmidt with his first wife, Karoline Perssin (1878 – around 1940), photographed in Vienna around 1900, a year after their marriage. She fell victim to mental illness and was confined to an asylum (intermittently to begin with, and permanently from 1919) until she was put to death by the Nazis, probably a year or so after Schmidt's own death.

major, bringing with it two subtle rhythmic changes to the lovely cadence before sliding back to D flat as easily as it left it, and gradually the easing balm of this music makes way for the return to the scherzo. This comes complete, but without the original indicated repetitions, and leads again to the theme of rising seconds which earlier brought the D flat music. This time it eases the music to its end in E major, the final syncopated *pizzicato* chords rising and vanishing like smoke.

Fourth Movement: Lebhaft, doch nicht zu Schnell

With the finale we resume an aspect of the work we have not had since the introduction to the first movement – the Baroque style. The movement is contrapuntal to a great extent, but not primarily fugal, although fugue plays a part. It is more like an enlarged Brandenburg Concerto movement, on a scale of size never used by Bach, but with a range of harmony not far in excess of what the older composer might have used. And, most important, whether or not the piece was composed before the rest of the work, as one hears the Symphony this movement appears as the natural outcome of the rest.

The $\frac{3}{2}$ phrases have a seventeenth- or early eighteenth-century connotation, although a Baroque composer probably would not have begun a theme with an upward leap of a major seventh, followed by a drop of a minor seventh, as Schmidt does. But a recurring cadence, in a number of versions, of which Ex. 16 shows two, is pure Baroque, yet fits the general

Ex. 16

surroundings admirably. There is another virtue in Schmidt's having chosen a three-beat time for this movement, which could so easily have raced away, individual notes at the same speed, at two minim beats to the bar. The extra beat per bar puts a necessary brake on the suggested speed (to the ear) of the fastest notes, altough the actual beat speed is no different. In fact, for the first four bars, unless the accentuation in performance is very carefully done, it could be a two-minim time. It is from bar 5 onwards that the brake is applied, and even so, there is still a danger that the quaver speed could

Ex. 17

overrun the music. As we shall see, Schmidt has provided against that.

The theme itself, with its harmony, suggests immediately (Ex. 17) the beginning of a late-nineteenth-century version of a Baroque concerto movement, as I have already implied, and is thus, with the movement as a whole, in line with the Jensen and d'Albert suites I have discussed (the Dohnányi came later). When the theme breaks into quaver movement, in bar 5, the likeness becomes still more pronounced; and yet the true period of this music is never for a moment in doubt. Ex. 17 is taken to the dominant, with further expansion of the quaver answer, and the music comes to E minor with a new quaver theme on violins with beautifully placed subsidiary figures on woodwind. The harmony moves with true Baroque steadiness – the slowness that is apparent in the fastest Baroque piece, as compared to Classically fast movement, a slowness that is inherent in the nature of extended counterpoint – and Ex. 17 is gradually re-introduced, hovering round G major, with a prominent version in that key of the cadence shown in Ex. 16a. The quaver continuation is developed further, with more and more subsidiary wind figures. G major, however, relapses to the dominant of E minor, and in that key Ex. 17, with two intervals changed to adapt its character to the minor key, begins a double *fugato*, with a new countersubject using the Ex. 16b version of the cadence with the end of the two-bar subject, and a new development (Ex. 18) of the quaver continuation figure. The balance between

late-nineteenth-century harmonic style and Baroque-type
passage work and movement is as nearly perfectly maintained
as makes no difference.

Ex. 18

It will be noticeable that there is no attempt so far in this
movement (nor is there in what remains) to make of it a
sonata-style movement or rondo; nor, except for one episode,
is there recourse to the other favourite for a classical finale –
variation. What does crop up, in the course of the *fugato*, is a
theme with a tail of two notes (Ex. 19) which becomes
important later, in conjunction with Ex. 18. The figure of a
second, Ex. 19a, becomes more prominent only a few bars
later as the basis of a counterpoint to Ex. 17, when the music
heads for a climactic statement by violins of Ex. 17 firmly in G
major, with impressive support from lower strings, trumpets,
trombones and tuba. This passage closes with the strongest
version of Ex. 16a we have yet had, the extra strength being
partly supplied by an extension of the first of the two intervals
from a sixth to a seventh; a very simple cadence, but
emphatic – and that is the point. It is one more piece of the
Baroque picture this movement is forming.

Ex. 19

So far from there being any connection with sonata style,
the only tonal moves have been those from one harmony of the
key to another, exactly as one would expect in a Baroque
movement. From E major we have moved to its dominant,
back to the tonic, which became minor, to G major, back to E
minor, a touch of C major moving on again to G major; and
this brings us up to date. And all these, let me repeat, except
for E major and minor, are harmonies visited as parts of the

key of E, the tonic of which is never far away and always to be sensed in the background when not actually present. In other words, tonally the movement has behaved exactly like any Baroque movement of reasonable size.

And now there appears, on woodwind and horns, what, it seems to me, everything has been waiting for. I said earlier that Schmidt had provided against the fairly rapid quaver movement overrunning the music and this new idea is what he has provided; or, rather, it is one half of it. It is a chorale, the one Tschulik finds 'not fully convincing' (it is idle to speculate why, for he has been shy of giving us a reason), but with it (Ex. 20) everything takes on a new and larger dimension. At

Ex. 20

the close of the chorale Ex. 17 breaks out still in G major, and with a new joyousness in its sound. From the start of its answer it is over a pedal dominant, and that answer itself receives a slight extension which simultaneously deepens its character and leads to a series of sequences which fall gradually to a resumption of the chorale, this time by *pizzicato* strings against a running quaver counterpoint on oboe and bassoon. Although we have not yet heard the full scope of the material of this movement, Ex. 20 slots into place as a sort of coping-stone to the rest, particularly since its two appearances so far are quiet and unassuming.

Halfway through this second statement of the chorale the quaver counterpoint is transferred to the violins, the *pizzicato* of the lower strings reinforced by sustained chords on clarinets and bassoon. The end of this chorale statement releases a cadence theme on a flute, the violins' pattering quavers continuing. The cadence theme reaches back to Ex. 18, the new development of the quaver continuation of Ex. 17, for the rising scale of five quavers which begins that development also sets off the cadence theme of Ex. 21. Over a long pedal G the

Ex. 21

cadence theme droops gradually lower and lower in pitch, the
quavers continuing. These even manage to contain a variation
of the theme as a counterpoint to it, and the variation subtly
turns into a diminished version of Ex. 17. Eventually the
quavers are left quite alone as they move to initiate a new
stage in the movement, a stage which is, in fact, an extension
of them in a totally new character.

From the approach to the chorale the music has been on (or
in) G major. I put it this way because: (a) the music came to
G from E minor, and G is the so-called relative major of E
minor, so that they are, in fact, parts of the same key, and
normally the tonic of E would not be interfered with; (b) this
will operate only if the excursion to the particular harmony is
brief; (c) if that excursion is extended, gradually it takes over
and its own tonic – G in this instance – becomes for the time
being the tonic to our ears. That has happened in this case. It
is a gentle, undramatic process, and has no relationship to the
dramatic key change which operates in the Classical sonata
and works derived from that structure (a dramatic key change
which *can* be found in the first movement of this Symphony)
and, indeed, was the only way in which, temporarily, the key
sense was ever changed in a Baroque piece of music – by
gentle insistence.

G major has already been extended long enough to begin to
dominate the music. But it is to be extended still further.
Schmidt now gives us the other half of his bulwark against too
much haste in this finale and, surprisingly, it turns out to be
the fastest thing in the movement. But perhaps this is not so
surprising as it may at first seem. The chorale has applied a
brake to hold back and control the speed of the music, and if
that is to be fully tested it needs the other extreme as well.
Wisely Schmidt has chosen a different kind of fast speed for
this interlude, and one that is easier to control, since it has
simple half-bar beats that are easily marked. It is the first

appearance in his work of a style that was to be developed as a definite feature of his later music. It is a matter of fairly rapid (actual speeds vary) pattering notes in a time with notes in groups of three, either $\frac{3}{4}$ or $\frac{6}{8}$, usually in a definite counterpoint. Examples in later works are the scherzo and Variation VI in the finale of the A major String Quartet (1925), the finale of the Quintet (1926) for piano and strings in G major, to some extent the scherzo of the Second String Quartet (1929), in part in the ninth variation (acting as scherzo) in the middle movement of the Second Symphony (1911–13), the scherzo of the Fourth Symphony (1932–33), and at a somewhat slower tempo the scherzo of the Third Symphony (1927–28). In a different time, $\frac{2}{4}$, there is also the ninth variation in the *Concertante Variations on a Theme of Beethoven* for piano (left hand) and orchestra of 1923. In this first instance

Ex. 22

(Ex. 22) it appears as another Baroque feature, a gigue in the style of a *fugato*, which is also the one connection with variation I mentioned earlier; it is a variation of Ex. 17. At first, and throughout a four-voice exposition, it is for strings only. Woodwind join in as the music becomes momentarily harmonic instead of contrapuntal, thus demonstrating that he is not writing a fugue proper. After a due harmonic assertion of the dominant the *fugato* continues with a minor version of the subject of Ex. 22, and gradually the music swings round towards E minor. Eventually the beginning of Ex. 17 is heard on half-bar beats, dotted crotchets, first on bassoons, then horn, as E swings on to the subdominant of E major and builds up to a return of Ex. 17 at the original tempo in full E major. The dotted-crotchet hints at Ex. 17 actually come at very nearly the original tempo, so that they, in this way, are also preparations for the return, and also mark the fundamental steadiness in this fastest music in the movement. All the subsidiaries return also, and with some modifications the music is kept to E major, to swing on to the chorale, much more fully scored in the brass, full-throated with quaver and crotchet counterpoints resounding around it. Further development of the subsidiary figures forms a fair-sized coda, and the Symphony comes to an impressively triumphant end.

As with the styles used in the first movement, the orchestration is a curious mixture of elements which does not produce what would seem to be the obvious result (a mess) but instead does produce a homogeneous whole. With the introduction we have a mainly Classical-type orchestra, admittedly with a double-bassoon, a third trumpet, three trombones and a bass tuba, which nonetheless conveys a very convincing effect of the beginning of a French overture. The unusual depth of tone does not sound incongruous, but majestic. Naturally, it is a *tutti*. The rising trumpet leading to the beginning of the main movement, and the horns that begin it, bring a momentary Romantic touch, but the *tutti* outburst that follows is purely classical. With the drift towards the second group the same orchestra provides a definite later 19th-century Romanticism, particularly in the use of the massed strings on rising and falling arpeggios, changing harmony in mid-flow. There is, coming from the whole Symphony, a certain opulence of sound which is kept under tight control, and one of the most remarkable features of the work is not only how a variety of styles is moulded to a homogeneous result, but also how this is reflected in, and contributed to, by the orchestration; the one goes with, or echoes, the other.

That the First Symphony is still so infrequently played, even where Schmidt's music is most performed, while the other three gain in number of performances, is part of the reason (the other part is simply lack of intelligent musical attention) that it is misunderstood on the rare occasions it is discussed at all; and also the reason that most of his later music rarely gets the understanding it deserves. The First Symphony is the key to the whole. Schmidt here defined his position as a serious symphonist. It was a position he was to consolidate.

III. SYMPHONY NO. 2 IN E FLAT MAJOR
(1911–13)

The first three Symphonies came at long intervals. That between the Second and Third was filled with the production of other music, but from the First to the Second there is only one major work, the opera *Notre Dame*. He did in 1904 write a 'Lied, Ländler und Marsch' for nine wind instruments and drums, with the title *Tullnerbacher Blasmusik*, written for the family of Alexander Wunderer.[1] It was eventually published by Doblinger in Vienna in 1975. It is the only listed work apart from the opera, and the latter was completed in 1904, although it was not performed until 1914. So from 1904 until 1911, when Schmidt began to work on the Second Symphony, he was virtually silent as a composer, it seems; and there was a reason for this.

This period brought Schmidt a great deal of worry and aggravation, connected with his position as a cellist in the Vienna Philharmonic Orchestra, of which Mahler was then conductor. I am not here going to recount the details of the quarrel and misunderstanding between Mahler and Schmidt, which was fanned by Arnold Rosé, the leader, and which led eventually to Schmidt's leaving the orchestra. They can be read in Schmidt's *Autobiographical Sketch*,[2] where the story is fully told. That Mahler, in his dealings with the orchestra, was an autocrat we know. Therefore, that he behaved autocratically goes without saying. Those on the receiving end had much to bear, and Schmidt, whether or not he acted foolishly, was one of them. For whatever reason, he allowed a lot of dust to settle after Mahler rejected *Notre Dame* in 1904 before he tackled his next major work. Partly as a result of this conflict, partly because of his teaching commitment at the Vienna Academy, Schmidt had originally intended to leave the

[1] See footnote 3 on p. 13.
[2] Appendix. pp. 176–178.

Vienna Philharmonic Orchestra in 1907, but he did not do so until April 1911, and even then retained his membership of the Court Orchestra. But note the effect, which tells us more of the restriction imposed during this seven-year period than anything else could: almost as soon as he left the orchestra he began work on the Second Symphony. This was the last non-productive gap in his career. (Production certainly slowed down towards the end of his life, but that was due to severe illness, a different matter altogether.)

Nonetheless, in spite of a twelve-year gap from the completion of the First Symphony to his starting work on the Second, there was a link in the opera, for *Notre Dame* is a very symphonic work (without being in the least Wagnerian). In fact, it gave him an opportunity to test the lyricism that was natural to him in surroundings where drama came to meet him – on the stage. It is drama of a very different kind from that of the symphony or sonata but drama nonetheless, and the intermixing of the two can only have had a very beneficial effect upon his symphonic outlook, when the E flat Symphony came along some seven years later. The experience had matured him, in spite of external conflicts; these may even have helped.

In discussing the First Symphony I have noted (and I think it will have become evident even in the quotations) that Schmidt was a composer in whom the lyrical was foremost among his creative gifts, and that the dramatic aspect had to be made out of that lyrical side. Other composers have been faced with this problem: some, like Schubert, Schumann and, to a certain extent, Brahms (in whom the problem was only partially present) successfully reconciled the two, each in his own way; others have not – Grieg and Rachmaninov are but two. Schmidt, too, was successful in negotiating this problem. In the First Symphony the first movement, the only part of the work which is dramatic in a Classical sense and which follows an introduction already Baroque in style, begins with lyrical material on the horns and only then goes on to a theme which has the makings of Classical drama within it. And, while keeping a sufficient balance throughout, at every new stage of the movement it is the lyrical which gets first hearing. Given that Schmidt was naturally a lyrical composer, this is what one might expect; what is interesting (since this is, so far as we know, his first major fling as a composer) is the subtlety with which he maintains the balance and presents us with a movement the symphonically dramatic nature of which is never in doubt.

Composers who have shared this problem with Schmidt and failed to master it often show their inexpertness, apart from the matter of the material and the handling of it, in the matter of dramatic tonality, which is essential to the dramatic nature of sonata (and symphonic) music. Here, too, Schmidt shows no hesitation in that First Symphony, in which we have seen his mastery of the tonality required for this kind of music, although how he had acquired or developed it to this degree we do not know.

Schmidt is so far true to his nature that, with one exception, in every sonata work he wrote (that we possess) he begins with the lyrical in material and then passes to what will aid the dramatic movement of the piece. (The exception, and it is so only in part, is the Fourth Symphony, but we shall come to it in due course.)

The orchestra employed in the Second Symphony is considerably larger than that of the First. Although the First had three bassoons, and the third doubling double-bassoon, and the Second has two and a double-bassoon, the E flat Symphony has three flutes instead of two, as well as piccolo, cor anglais, E flat clarinet, three B flat clarinets, bass clarinet, eight horns instead of four, and a battery of percussion – and yet for some reason the First sounds opulent compared with the Second, although the orchestra in the First is handled with restraint. Nonetheless, in spite of its extra instruments and generally larger-scale orchestration, the Second has often a lean, muscular sound which fits its character admirably. This is not because of less material (rather, there is more) but partly because the additional instruments are rarely used for doubling; and the opulent sound of the First Symphony is a good deal due to late nineteenth-century orchestration of material that is either Baroque or Classical in style.

First Movement: Lebhaft

The Second Symphony is also concerned with the Baroque, although to a much less extent than its predecessor. The first movement begins with a theme (Ex. 23a) which is lyrical and

Ex. 23

has Baroque connotations in that it is, in style, very like a characteristic Bach type of instrumental, even keyboard, theme (there has been conjecture that Schmidt began this work as a possible piano sonata). On the face of it, Ex. 23a has far less pretension as a suitable symphonic theme than anything in the first movement of the E major work, yet it helps to build a more persuasive symphonic movement. Not that it is left to do this on its own – Schmidt was too wise for that – for it is here a case of the gradual infiltration of Ex. 23a. Part of its importance is that it sets a scene, touched with Schmidt's own sound colour (rather as, with a different but equally personal colouring, the solo cello in C major at the beginning of Tovey's Cello Concerto sets a much longer lyrical scene to prepare the dramatic onslaught of the full orchestra in C minor); but that is not the sum of the importance of Ex. 23a. The semiquaver figures that grow out of it also sometimes suggest a dotted rhythm, as Exx. 23b and c show; in fact, Ex. 23c already has the semiquavers leading to a jerky rhythm (which for convenience I will call dotted, although the dot is here replaced by a semiquaver rest); it is a rhythm of great dramatic importance in the movement, and it has grown out of the lyrical semiquaver theme. Schmidt did far more than present us with a fascinating lyrical theme when he designed Ex. 23a. And there is yet another aspect of Ex. 23a to which I will refer later.

For the moment the score is permeated with Ex. 23a and derivatives, two of which are a descending crotchet figure and a descending figure of broken quavers, of both of which we shall also hear more. The harmony is pitched round the tonic and dominant of E flat for some thirteen bars, and then moves quite naturally to the subdominant, which we might expect, from which the reaction is E major harmony, which at this point we do not expect. Its function is quite clear to the ear; it is a detour to establish E flat the more firmly by leaning on it. Properly speaking, it should be spelt as F flat, but E major is easier to read.

As the music shifts back from the local E major to the fundamental E flat, with the dominant in the bass, the dotted rhythm first heard explicitly in Ex. 23c, which has been gaining power, produces a theme (Ex. 24) of which we shall hear more, and with semiquavers becoming more and more

Ex. 24

excited and the dotted rhythm, in oboes and horns, cellos and bass, growing in a great crescendo, the music swings fully on to the tonic of E flat with a theme fundamental to the movement, the apotheosis of the dotted rhythm. It begins (Ex. 25) in the bass (on later evidence) and continues in upper parts.

Ex. 25

There is one thing in particular that stands out in all this opening part of the movement: in spite of the lyrical beginning the character of the music, without fuss or sudden change, has radically expanded and altered in a process of organic growth set in motion by the semiquaver groups that had hidden in them the dotted rhythm. This is part of Schmidt's solution to the dramatic problem; the opening lyrical idea has set off the beginning of the dramatic process. And this is the unmistakable mark of a symphonist.

Ex. 25 puts the symphonic crown on the whole of this beginning. From this point we are heading away from E flat and towards – well, what comes. What that will be we do not know yet. The semiquavers are still ubiquitous for some bars yet to come, Ex. 25 passes through E major for a moment, followed by G major, equally briefly, and the music marches steadily onward, just as though we were nearing our objective, a new key to replace E flat. But in Schmidt's scheme of things more is yet required to make this effective.

Chromaticism is a part of his language, as it was of the language of all nineteenth-century composers and a good many of the twentieth, each with his own accent. There are two basic aspects to chromaticism, the purely colourful and the diatonic. The diatonic, with essential help from an ally that is *not* chromatic, will aid in losing a key already established. The purely colouristic will only serve to emphasise an existing key the more firmly. It is *context* that imparts one or the other of these two characters to a chromatic passage. We are coming now to a passage (Ex. 26) which, one might think from the sound of it, is firmly and none too gently smashing its way away from E flat, to make it possible for the music to move elsewhere. There would appear to be nothing new about the idea of the overlapping entries in Ex. 26 – all that has been done before – or the type of rising bass, and yet the whole passage is so redolent of Schmidt's voice and accent, to the exclusion of those of anyone else, that if I wanted to demonstrate by just one passage to anyone unfamiliar with his sound exactly what it is like, this is the one I would choose. It is quite unlike anything in any other composer. The ingredients are simple enough: the overlaps, with their harshness of entry, the

Ex. 26

rising bass and the use of augmented triads; all had been used before by composers who never sound like this. What, therefore, makes the sound of Ex. 26 so special? We are here up against the magic of personality and context – and that is as far as words can go. The only explanation is the sound of the music, and that, like all intangibles, does not explain. It is simply satisfyingly and excitingly itself.

It can be seen (or, better still, heard) that at the end of Ex. 26 the music is moving in a peculiar direction if its object is to move away from E flat, for in spite of the chromatic push the bass note is E flat, and all the harmonic movement above indicates that the B flat is the dominant of E flat. And three and a half bars later the music arrives in a crescendo on E flat – but minor, not major: and the chromaticism for the last few bars, it can be heard now, has been urging E flat minor. The semiquavers have reappeared, and E flat minor is gained with a minor version of Ex. 23a, spread out over six beats, then four, and four more, as the volume diminishes.

E flat minor is important here. It might seem at first as though we had set out on a journey, encountered evidence on the way that we were approaching our goal, only to find that we have arrived back to a starting-point only very slightly different from when we left it. In fact, we have come a good deal further than that. We are on a brink or precipice, and what we are to tumble into is already two-thirds present in that E flat minor chord. So much is achieved by widely moving chromaticism and a change of one note in a common chord.

A few bars later Schmidt changes the key signature to one of five sharps, and from a pedal E flat the bass becomes a pedal F sharp. The change brings with it a new theme, but not one with the character of a main second group item. Rather, the

air is full of rustlings and flutterings, which give the music an
ephemeral air and prevent the stability the music is seeking.
The theme is based on an augmented triad and the fluttering
support makes use of the same harmony, before it grinds
semitonally against the F sharp, and passes on to a double-
dotted descending figure which is accompanied by rapidly
oscillating shakes for richly divided strings backed by woodwind. The whole, which occupies only a few bars in a slightly
retarded tempo, is like an echo of some of the music in *Notre
Dame*. Eventually the music closes back on to B major and we
hear the main second group tune played by a horn, the tempo
back to normal.

Now we can grasp the full import of that E flat minor
harmony. E flat and G flat are enharmonically D sharp and F
sharp. The B flat has only to rise one semitone and we have
the chord of B major. It is not done as simply as that, but that
is basically what has happened.

Ex. 27

Ex. 27a gives the second group tune as it is played for the
second time by first violins, with a counterpoint for second
violins. The counterpoint appears at its simplest with the
original horn statement, but in Ex. 27a it is very much
developed, and includes a turn which became an important
part of Schmidt's language (it had already made itself felt in
Notre Dame), as those who know the Fourth Symphony will be
well aware. Twice the tune has been heard in full B major. At
the end of this second statement it sweeps up on to D major
harmony for a third appearance on woodwind, horns, cellos

and second violins, the counterpoint still further developed; and it is the counterpoint in this third version which leads to the second and final part of the tune, shown in Ex. 27b. This is a development of the figure shown in the first half of the fourth bar of the tune in Ex. 27a, and forms a descending coda to the tune. Its falling process is arrested and turned into a further climb, bringing with it another (Ex. 28) of Schmidt's characteristic features. Ex. 15, from the scherzo of the First Symphony, had already hinted at this type of idea. It carries with

Ex. 28

it some of Schmidt's Hungarian expression (a strain which had already come to the fore in this way in the *Intermezzo* – Schmidt called it a *Zwischenspiel*, although it is generally known by the Italian title – from *Notre Dame*, and in other parts of the same opera); here, in Ex. 28, it turns into the third and fourth bars of Ex. 27a, bringing an even stronger climax on Ex. 27b. This completes its descent this time, becoming calmer, to come to rest on the tonic of B major, and a quiet, peaceful cadence theme to the exposition, an augmented version (Ex. 29) of the beginning of Ex. 23a (in quavers) which drops a little tail, marked *a*.

Ex. 29

An aspect of Ex. 27a which has a bearing on Schmidt's melodic style in general concerns its use of gradually widening intervals. On a smaller scale this can already be found in Ex. 23a. There are many later examples.[3]

The harmony changes to B minor for the final chord of the exposition, and from this a kettledrum provides a two-bar link to the development, first in the dotted rhythm of which we have heard so much, then in repeated semiquavers, all on B until the last half-bar, when it drops to B flat.

The tail (Ex. 29, fig. a) shows a type of interval movement with which Schmidt became increasingly pre-occupied – that of rising or falling fourths, sometimes perfect (as here), sometimes diminished. Here it immediately acquires a larger importance. The development begins as though we are to have a repetition of the exposition, which would be surprising but not impossible for a movement on this scale; but the cast of the music does not suggest such a likelihood. Although we have Ex. 23a and all its follow-up exactly as at the beginning of the movement (even with the same scoring), that this is no repetition is immediately put beyond doubt by the addition of a new figure (Ex. 30) on oboes and horns.

Ex. 30

This music is very susceptible to ideas. Schmidt has no sooner let Ex. 29 reveal its tail, fig. a, itself derived from Ex. 29 or even from Ex. 23a, than he begins to use it, for Ex. 30 is simply a greatly augmented version of that tail, the augmentation altering its whole character, giving it a masterful poise and dignity the original could never possess. For nine bars the music follows the course of the opening of the movement, Ex.

[3] Organists who know the huge E flat Prelude and Fugue of 1924 will recognise the same device in the Prelude's main theme; and it crops up again in the finale of the Second String Quartet of five years later, where it appears as the closing theme of the exposition, divided between violin and viola and summed up by the cello.

30 developing its own steady and controlling counterpoint to the rest. At that point, where the original climaxed on the tonic major, flats now intervene to turn the climax to E flat minor, with Ex. 23a in full voice and Ex. 29 adapting itself to the new harmony.

E flat minor harmony has already fulfilled one function in this movement – that of helping to bring the music within range of B major. Now it is used to help bring about another change of tonal direction, and a very important one. There are three main tonal areas in this movement – E flat (the basic key of the whole), B major (the key of the second group), and G major; and of the latter two G major is the more important, as events prove. The 'repetition' continues, Ex. 30 trailing a continuation in counterpoint with it, and we come to a touch of E major harmony, just as we heard it immediately prior to Ex. 24; there it acted as a 'leaning' harmony on E flat, to dig in that tonality the more firmly. Now Schmidt has another use for it, this time to move the music away from E flat, and Ex. 24 comes on G major, leading, as it did before, to Ex. 25.

But however much the foregoing may suggest that we are having a recapitulation with an added detail, that is *not* what it sounds like. The impression of *growth* and additional impact is overwhelming, and is reinforced when Ex. 25 drags a descending chromatic coda which plunges into the second group tune (Ex. 27a) on B minor, against a counterpoint formed from an extension of the first bar of Ex. 25. The Hungarian accent of Ex. 28 follows Ex. 27a again, pushing up the music this time to regain the three-flat key-signature, but on C minor, not E flat major. Ex. 25 is still the text, restricted to its first bar and a dotted-rhythm figure projected from it, which produces a quaver tail, C, B natural, A natural, B natural, repeating itself and gradually lengthening and eventually silencing the music, all over a pedal E flat, which is at last left rumbling quietly on a kettledrum.

A moment's silence brings the reaction – A flat major, and one of the most beautiful passages Schmidt ever wrote: the quaver enlargement of Ex. 23a, just as we heard it at the close of the exposition, but here expanding into a wonderful piece of non-fugal three-part counterpoint, for second violins, violas and cellos. For eleven and a half bars this expands, and then proves to be ushering in Ex. 27a. There is here an extra radiance about this tune, which develops through B major (its original harmony), giving this statement a sheen which quite eclipses its first appearance in this key. The music moves on to Ex. 27b, as before, but three bars of this bring a complete change of mood, as with a crescendo we move on to F minor and Ex. 27a, with the counterpoint formed from the first bar of Ex. 25. We have already heard this with the B minor version of Ex. 27a, but not with the devastating sound of this F minor version. For a moment the music seems to look ahead to the mid-1930s and some of the most frightening moments of the oratorio, *Das Buch mit Sieben Siegeln.*

The Hungarian sound reappears and, in a great crescendo, helps to push the music on to four chords (Ex. 31) for trumpets and horns, in which the horns increase by two until all eight are present and which are of gathering intensity and dissonance, each one separated from the next by a bar

Ex. 31

swamping the 'resolution' of the brass chord with Ex. 27b on top, and underneath a descending dotted rhythm and a mad rush of strings. It can be seen that the upper notes of the chords form each time a falling second. This interval here looks both backward and forward – backward to the beginning of Ex. 25, forward to a prominent theme in the finale, and the progressions shown in Ex. 31 form a sort of fulcrum. This is all still pitched on F, with kettledrum rolls adding emphasis, and at last the music passes through two bars on the dominant of E flat, to collapse on to a minor ninth for full wind over a D. From this, and the falling second, emerges one of the passages for wind alone that are a feature in later Schmidt, chromatically descending and again looking ahead, this time to certain passages in the Fourth Symphony. As it descends it diminishes in volume, and casts up a theme (Ex. 32) compounded

Ex. 32

of elements from Ex. 27a and Ex. 25. The music comes to rest on D major harmony, over a pedal D on kettledrum, and this is eventually left alone, except for four soft vibrations from the tamtam, leading to complete silence.

This development is not inordinately long, but it is huge – and the effect of development, of growth, of gradual change, is all around us as the music dies out to silence. We have been through a cataclysmic experience which leaves us with a mixture of moods, from the calm to the tempestuous, and a touch of the tragic. It is almost with a shock that the silence is broken by the quiet voice of Ex. 23a, as we heard it at the beginning of the development, with one difference – it is in G major, not E flat.

Some people, including me, talk of one key being brighter than another, and I think it can be heard without perfect pitch. Others deny this. A simple test for the latter is to compare the sound of the two versions of Schubert's E flat Piano Sonata, D.568. He wrote it first in D flat major, and later rewrote it in E flat. Even allowing for the fact that the pitch he knew was somewhat different from ours, you have only to play the two openings to hear the relatively brighter sound of the E flat version against that of the D flat. And I think it would be difficult for anyone with any response to the sound of music to hear this G major version of Ex. 23a, in a movement where pitch is constant anyway, without realising that it is altogether brighter than its original in E flat. This is partly by contrast with what has immediately preceded it, of course, but this does not entirely explain it. I do not think that anyone could hear this passage, having heard all that has led to it, and believe we have arrived home, tonally. It is a recapitulation in all but key, reinforced by the fact that this time there is no extra detail (Ex. 30). But the mood it engenders is its own; something gained, a complete justification of the development.

The recapitulation proceeds, moving through a touch of C major harmony changing to A flat, Ex. 24 sounds as A flat gives way to B, and the music swirls up on the dominant of B, prepared for Ex. 25 on B major. And here Schmidt gives us the outstanding momentary surprise of the movement, for that preparation sidesteps B and thunders out Ex. 25 back on G major, the F sharp simply shifting up a semitone, after a split second's breathless silence, one semiquaver long.

Everything now comes as before, but not sounding quite as it did originally. Even with a recapitulation in the basic key of the movement, exposition material can never sound exactly as it did before; too much has happened in between and if we are attentive listeners the effect of that music cannot help but affect the way in which we hear a recapitulation. In this case, in addition to what has happened since we heard the first group in the exposition, the very key we are in helps to make the difference. The music marches on through Ex. 26 and comes to G minor, replacing the original E flat minor, with the lengthened first bar of Ex. 23a; it comes eventually to the dominant of E flat, where before we had the dominant of B major. The new theme, the rustlings and flutterings, all come as before to lead the music to the second-group tune on violins in E flat major. We are home; an altered home, but home nonetheless. The whole second group follows, with different but equally full orchestration, right up to the drum notes (E flats now) that linked the exposition to the development. They link the recapitulation to the coda, this time without the drop of a semitone on the last half-bar. That is delayed to the end of the bar, where the coda begins with a sustained chord of B minor, the E flat of the drum thus dropping a semitone to the D of the chord.

Against the B minor chord, the tempo now much slower, the mood calmly brooding, Ex. 32 begins a gradual progress in the lower woodwind, in counterpoint with a derivative of Ex. 25, dwelt upon by second violins and violas, followed by woodwind, with first violins supplying a very quiet triplet background. After two of these double statements, the second a third higher in pitch, Ex. 23a is injected into the texture for three bars. This brings us to a grinding climax, the beginning of Ex. 25, on horns and trumpet, set between the extremes of a major seventh. It is carried up another step, this time on trombones and trumpets. Throughout the coda so far the bass has gradually risen, step by step, from the low B on which it started to the A a minor seventh above, partly diatonically, partly chromatically. As the bass reaches the A strings and horns play Ex. 27a on D major, with counterpoint involving the turn – not, however, the same as accompanied the second statement of this tune quoted in Ex. 27a. The music moves to a second statement on horns and clarinets pitched on F major, and on through C minor, with a bass suggesting Ex. 27a but which is not quite that idea; Ex. 23a swells above it *fortissimo*, and the remaining counterpoints that burgeoned around Ex. 27a in its original second and third statements are all here, moving on through the subdominant of E flat to E flat itself, with all the build up to Ex. 25, the semiquavers swirling throughout. At the very end G major again intrudes momentarily with Ex. 25 on brass, and with one flick of a beat we reach the final chord of E flat, snapped off as it sounds.

There is little more to say about this amazing piece; but if anyone wanted to know how a large dramatic symphonic movement could be evolved with mastery from material basically lyrical, here is an object lesson.

Second Movement: Einfach und Zart

Sonata style is not only concerned with dramatic tensions: since normally it breaks up into a number of pieces, or movements, it allows also for reactions from one movement to another – as, on a smaller scale, a single movement is concerned with reactions from one mood to another. In the work of attentive artists whose gifts fit them for the composition of sonata works, there is a rightness in the order of movements as they are presented in sonata or symphony, so

that interference with that order, or the making of cuts, which
some well-known performers are not above, immediately
spoils the finished result.[4]

Schmidt decided not to follow his massive first movement
with a customary slow movement and instead chose what
sounds like the perfect reaction – a theme and ten variations.
Ex. 33 gives the theme complete. It is an ideal basis for
variations, and, if the composer has a sure grip on them,
nothing can more certainly provide an inevitable growth of
tension, with plenty of opportunity to relax it when necessary.
But the touch must be right, and many composers have
essayed variations in sonata works who had not the right
touch. Schmidt's tune gives him all the opportunity he needs.

Ex. 33

Its simplicity is deceptive, for it has a strong but simple
harmonic framework which, as with any good tune, is already
evident in the tune alone; once he had written the tune,
Schmidt had only to cross the 't's and dot the 'i's harmonically.
His sets of variations are not many, in a comparatively small
output of works, but they are all masterly,[5] and this, the first,

---

[4] Mahler's Sixth Symphony is a curious exception, for it seems that to the
end of his life he could not make up his mind about the correct order for the
second and third movements.

[5] The others are the *Concertante Variations on a Theme of Beethoven* (1923) for
piano (left hand) and orchestra, the organ *Chaconne* (1925, orchestrated in
1931 – below, pp. 147–151), the *Adagio* of the Third Symphony (in a way –

is as fine as any of them.

Ex. 33 is for woodwind alone. It is but commonsense that the first variation is for strings, in beautiful flowing four-part counterpoint, the theme straightforwardly in first violins, and at the same tempo. Schmidt had the Classical composers' way of allowing his theme to sink in before becoming adventurous, a habit which can be found also in Brahms and as late as Reger.

One of Schmidt's most subtle habits is that of lengthening or shortening phrases, often by the merest fraction but sufficiently to affect the impact of the music. It is sometimes done by holding a note a little longer, or by shortening, or inserting a rest, or omitting one that was present. It is extraordinary how much personal aura can be imparted to a theme by these means. Ex. 33 is made up of an eight-bar phrase, then a six-bar and two more of eight bars. The effect of the six-bar length among the longer phrases is striking. But Schmidt adds to this in his first variation. The tune is precisely the same, the phrases come as in Ex. 33, but the last note of the penultimate eight-bar phrase is held a bar longer. That is all, but its effect is almost to make the tune sound a slightly different shape.

Var. II (*Etwas fliessender*) is the third passage in the work for wind alone, here woodwind and one horn. This is slightly faster than the theme and Var. I, the theme split up (Ex. 34)

Ex. 34

below, pp. 102–106), the orchestral *Variations on a Hussar Song* (1930–31), and the Finale, 'Variations on a Theme of Josef Labor', of the Quintet in A (1938) for clarinet and piano quartet.

between two little choirs, one of oboes, cor anglais and
bassoons, the other of clarinets, bass clarinet and horn. Once
again Schmidt takes liberties with that third phrase. Ex. 34a
shows the manner of dividing the tune; Ex. 34b what happens
at the end of the third phrase, expanded from eight to ten
bars, and not merely by extending the length of a single note.

Var. III (*Schnell und leicht*) applies to the strings the idea of
two little choirs with alternating interjections. Ex. 35a shows
the idea; Ex. 35b Schmidt's phrasing game taken further. Not
only does the third phrase retain its new ten-bar length, but
the six-bar second phrase is also extended to eight, the
extension caused by the circling round D flat, C and E flat at
what were the original third and fourth bars of that phrase.

Ex. 35

With Var. IV (*Schnell*) the whole thing (as far as we have
known it) goes sky high. The tempo has two minim beats to
the bar, each minim roughly the same length as one bar of
Var. III. This would seem to slow the music down; in fact, it
shoots it forward as though from a gun, partly because each
crotchet is spelt out in semiquavers by divided cellos and
bassoons, with timpanum marking each half bar. In format it
is the simplest variation in the whole set for, after two bars to
set the pace, the tune is reduced to a suggestion by semibreves
and minims, with subtle chromatic inflections (Ex. 36). In this
musical shorthand the original phrase-lengths have no meaning. The first happens still to be represented by eight bars, but
the second and third are reduced to four bars, and the final

Ex. 36

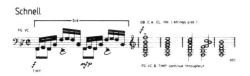

one to five, the ubiquitous semiquaver support left vigorously operating for another five bars. In the last two it becomes an oscillation of G flat and F, preparing for Var. V. Here (Ex. 37)

Ex. 37

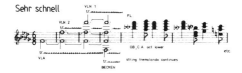

the key-signature changes from two to five flats for B flat minor, the tempo (*Sehr Schnell*) is a *Presto* $\frac{6}{8}$ and the whole variation is conveyed by two woodwind choirs over persistent string shakes, to which a cymbal adds a tremolando; this later gives way to a timpanum, which in turn hands back to the cymbal. The theme is more than suggested, but it takes on a strange distortion in these altered circumstances, as a rather demoniac *tarantella*, although the harmonies adapted to the minor key, keep it on course. Also, the phrases are all ironed out to four straight sets of eight bars; and, in these surroundings, following the various adventures the phrasing has had so far, this normal four-square proceeding has the effect of something slightly off-centre.

Var. V is the first of a block of three, Vars. VI and VII developing from V; this is a device which can be found prominently in some of the larger sets by Beethoven and Brahms. There is no break between them, but there is change of mood. Var. VI keeps the $\frac{6}{8}$ rhythm, but much slower (*Langsam und Ruhig*), and with a languishing lilt that suggests a barcarolle. A swaying figure derived from Ex. 37 supplies a background to the theme, now suggested in a song (Ex. 38) for flute, clarinet and violins. The phrasing, again, is much the same yet subtly different. For instance, because of the $\frac{6}{8}$ rhythm, many notes which were originally a crotchet in length become five quavers long, as can be seen in Ex. 38, and this adds to the spirit of the whole variation. But what intensifies it is that the lengthened notes sometimes are followed by the theme as it originally moved, in quavers. The whole is extremely subtle, and would alone mark Schmidt's gift for the variation as a vehicle for musical expression.

Ex. 38

Although Vars. V, VI and VII form a group, there is a short pause marked at the end of Var. VI, which serves to propel Var. VII with a greater intensity. The theme is given in two versions simultaneously, in $\frac{6}{8}$ and $\frac{2}{4}$, and the key has for the first time moved away from B flat, to E flat minor (Ex. 39).

Ex. 39

Now the key changes radically (though with a link between B flat and A sharp) to F sharp major and an outpouring of Schmidt's Hungarian style of passionate expression that could almost have strayed here from the *Intermezzo* from *Notre Dame*. Woodwind and strings interlock with each other to provide a completely reconceived version of the original theme. Ex. 40 gives first flute and first violins for the first phrase. To begin with, each of these lines has its own version of the overall melodic line, but the two coalesce to become one thing. But further, if you consider the first eight-bar phrase of Ex. 33 and then take the first note of each of the first two pairs of bars in Ex. 40, the first note in each of the fifth, sixth and seventh, and

Ex. 40

the same again for the second eight bars, you will find that you have a strong suggestion of that original first phrase. The rest of the theme is handled in similar fashion. But the *character* of this eighth variation is supplied by the interlacing passionate thematic work, with its full-throated harmony. At one point near the end the *Intermezzo* from *Notre Dame* is actually quoted (Ex. 41). True, it is only a matter of a rising third, bracketed in Ex. 41a and b, but that rising third has the same accent and meaning in each case; and it is evoked in this way, it seems, whenever Schmidt is in his Hungarian gypsy mood. It seems evident that this orchestral rhapsody, originally composed in 1902–03, in essence remained with him and at times demanded further outlet, for apart from this eighth variation the *Variations on a Hussar Song* for orchestra, composed in 1930–31, has an introduction, used again later in the work, which calls even more on that early orchestral piece.

Ex. 41

Var. IX, the longest in the movement, reverts to B flat, very simply using the F sharp major harmony as a springboard in the brief introduction, beginning with a quaver figure much in evidence in the scherzo proper, which sets the mood, pace and style for the ensuing variation. In spite of its coming where it does, as the ninth in a set of ten variations, this has some claim to be considered as possibly the largest scherzo in Schmidt's output. The initial F sharp is treated as dominant of B major, on which harmony the opening phrase appears, to be used as the Neapolitan sixth harmony of B flat major, where the phrase is repeated. That opening phrase is the beginning of Ex. 33, adapted (Ex. 42) to Schmidt's scherzo style and rhythm, and this, even more than in the First Symphony, is entirely his own.

Ex. 42

Instead of repeating what we have just heard literally, Schmidt does so by the harmonies, but replaces the theme with an adaptation of the flute, clarinet and violin song in Ex. 38. The phrase comes to rest on the dominant of B flat, with the cor anglais hinting at a further development based on bar 13 of Ex. 33, a hint which is reinforced by a repetition by flutes and clarinets. This leads to Ex. 42, now pitched round the dominant, repeated and lifted by a semitone (answering the original drop of a semitone?) and again brought to a conclusion on the harmony of B flat. The development from bar 13 of Ex. 33 is now taken further (Ex. 43), suggesting bars 9–14 of

Ex. 43

Ex. 33 combined with the rhythm from Ex. 42, a passage which oscillates between D major and F major harmonies, and comes to a climax from which pattering strings are reinforced by wind echoes of the rhythm we have just been hearing. This sweeps into a waltz figure which suddenly really becomes bars 9–14 of Ex. 33, pitched on D flat major, the harmony on which it appeared in Ex. 33; it leads almost casually to Ex. 42 still on D flat, veering towards the home dominant, where bars 17–22 of Ex. 33 sing out on violins, a thematic development which brings Ex. 42 in its train as easily as did the previous passage. Everything from Ex. 43, up to the pattering strings and rhythmic reinforcement, is repeated and suddenly we are in the midst of a device peculiar to Schmidt, used mostly to bring to an end something which otherwise suggests it could go on for ever: a sound, usually tonally based, but with a falling chromatic dissonance (plus, in this instance, rushing semiquavers – their first appearance in continuous movement in the scherzo), which suggests something disintegrating. We had a touch of it towards the end of Var. VIII, but this example strikes much deeper. It will be used again, in principle, for even deeper meaning in later works. Here at last it descends to Var. X, the last in this set, and, so far as it has one, the real slow movement of the work.

The lengthy, simple tune of Ex. 33 has been used, bit by bit and yet in the most connected way, as a text for one of the largest and most mature of Schmidt's scherzi, completely adapted to this style with phrases extended and repeated in a variety of ways. The result is that one is constantly kept guessing as to which is coming next, and in what manner. As with the scherzo of the First Symphony, there is a strong suggestion of the *Ländler* about it, the leisurely progress of that dance curiously mixed with the rapid urgency of a full-scale scherzo. (It is a mistake, incidentally, to stress unduly the *Ländler* aspect of this movement by taking it too steadily, as I have heard some conductors perform it. Such a slack tempo destroys the thing it tries to enhance, the *Ländler*; all it achieves is that the music, which should be freely moving all the time, is forced to drag, and this is disastrous.)

Ostensibly Var. X, in C sharp major, which begins with a *tremolando* ostinato on the cellos, acts as trio to the scherzo, albeit a very slow one; but there is not the slightest connection between the languorous movement and harmony of Schmidt's Var. X and the almost religious fervour of Bruckner's slow trios. As with Var. VIII, Schmidt may appear to have departed from his theme, even to have forgotten it. But, as was shown in that variation, he has it very much in mind. He is using the basic notes of the theme as a structure for a new melody – true variation writing. This basic shape can be traced throughout this lovely piece of writing, ostensibly so different from its original. Ex. 44 shows the new melodic structure, of which one is mainly aware, and above it the outline of the tune adapted to the ⅜ rhythm. This type of procedure can be traced at least as far back as the slow movement of Beethoven's Ninth Symphony, although there the new tune is more in the nature of elaborate decoration of the variation theme; nonetheless, it has the effect of a new

Ex. 44

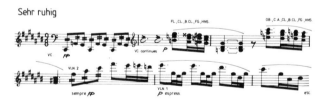

melodic line. In Schmidt's Var. X we can hear once again momentary echoes of the Hungarian gypsy strain from *Notre Dame*. At the end the *tremolando* ostinato of the cellos is left sounding alone, except for a last wisp of the Var. X melody.

As at the beginning of Var. IX, an introduction, similar to the original, leads to the resumption of the scherzo – not, however, in the same harmonic direction at first. We are now coming from C sharp major, not the F sharp major of Var. VIII. By the time we get to the adaptation of the flute song from Ex. 38 we are back on the original pitch, B flat major, and the whole scherzo follows as before, to the point where the music led to Var. X. Since the trio is not to be repeated,

Schmidt's repetition of the scherzo expands in an accelerating coda, turning his falling chromatic chords to rising ones, adapting them to the increased pace with devastating effect, and maintaining the scherzo mood and quaver movement to the end. In the last five bars cellos and basses, horn and tuba give a hint (which might be accidental) of Ex. 23 from the first movement.

The orchestration in this repetition of the scherzo is not always the same as in the original. Some of the texture is lightened, some passages are set lower in pitch than before, and the resulting contrasts are welcome and add to the impressiveness of the whole conception. Formally, the movement balances beautifully between first movement and finale; it is poised with the delicate precision which keeps a huge boulder securely in place on an apparently inadequate pedestal. Schmidt's technical engineering here was absolutely accurate.

Third Movement: Finale. Langsam – Ruhig und Fliessend

What kind of finale could follow two such movements? I wonder what we would expect, having reached that point in listening to this Symphony for the first time. There is no difficulty as far as the first movement is concerned; the problem is with the variations. If we had heard a straightforward slow movement followed by a scherzo we might well expect a fairly normal fast finale, perhaps a rondo. And we have just heard a slow movement and a scherzo (or a slow movement mixed up with a scherzo, which makes a difference); but we have heard other things, too. The whole does not add up to a 'normal' reaction to the first movement, although it is 'correct' on Schmidt's own terms. At this point we might well be left scratching our heads, especially since the end of the previous movement is so like Schmidt's favourite way of ending a work: his favourite device of sharp final chord, ending a thematic statement, and with an immediate cut-off (although he had done this at the end of the first movement, it does not reduce the effect at the end of the second). We might say that such spirited energy as ends that movement needs time for recuperation and thus should expect at least a slow introduction. And it could well be that – what we hear appears (Ex. 45) to be fairly slow-moving fugal writing for wind. At any rate, if not fugal (as it proves not to be), it is polyphonic, and as the piece progresses it becomes evident that we are hearing some of the finest wind polyphony ever imagined.

Ex. 45

It is of some importance here (and even more later) that the theme in the first bar and a half of Ex. 45 contains the melodic shape of the first four bars of Ex. 33, minus the upbeat, compressed into one short figure, and adapted by the change of one note (G to G flat) to E flat minor. Indeed, the connection can be taken further back: it can be seen (and heard) that this figure actually grows from those shown in Ex. 23, made even clearer in Ex. 29, and the new wind figure derived from this at the beginning of the development in the first movement, Ex. 30. It can now be appreciated that, so far as the Symphony as a whole is concerned, the variation theme grows out of that initial material of the first movement. In addition, of course, Ex. 42 is also Ex. 45 a fifth higher and with a different rhythm, so that the material for the connection is stressed right up to the end of the movement – to the point where the finale begins. And (as if to stress this still more) at the very end of the second movement, at the height of the acceleration, close listening can detect the first horn playing Ex. 45 at precisely that pitch, and with no frills, minus only the lengthened note it begins with.

The movement of the parts is remarkably like that of sixteenth-century polyphony,[6] although the harmony

---

[6] *Cf.* Oskar Adler's remark to Schmidt, quoted on p. 16.

produced is not remotely of that century. The great mass of
moving lines lingeringly moves from the tonic of E flat minor,
through a touch of G flat, to the minor dominant, where, after
a crescendo, the music quietens down to a drawn-out cadence
on B flat minor. Here, on a quietly rich G flat major, the
strings intervene with a new theme, which has the effect of
moving faster because, where the previous passage has moved
only by minims and crotchets, the new idea moves mainly on
crotchets and quavers, in flowing counterpoint. It is quiet,
grave, extremely beautiful, and it has Schmidt's personality
stamped all over it. Pitched (except for one quaver deviation)
over a pedal G flat, it occupies only nineteen bars, compared
with the thirty-five of the first part of the movement, but it is
weighty with an importance not yet disclosed when the
woodwind re-enter, overlapping by three bars. However,
towards the end of the nineteen-bar period a particularly
beautiful melodic line (Ex. 46) is released by the violins. The
wind re-enter with an inversion (Ex. 47) of the theme from Ex.

Ex. 46

Ex. 47

45; which proves to be more important and proportionately
more compelling to the ear than its original right side up, so
much so that one remembers Ex. 47 as the right side up rather
than Ex. 45, even though in this re-entry of the wind Ex. 45 is
soon heard in the general polyphonic mêlée. Nearly every
entry – and the piece is in constant *stretto* – brings a new
continuation; the harmony veers to B flat minor, thence
momentarily to A flat minor and, over a solid augmentation of
the answer to Ex. 45 on bassoon, double-bassoon and horns,

back to E flat minor and the final full peroration to this part of
the movement. In the last few bars the harmony smoothes out
to E flat major and we slide easily into the finale proper. The
theme we are given could make us wonder still more what
kind of finale this is going to be. It is Ex. 46 – Schmidt at his
most lyrical.

We have encountered by now enough of Schmidt's methods
to realise that such a lyrical beginning to the main movement
(or the larger part of what may be considered as one
movement, in the light of later events) does not by any means
preclude some type of dramatic sonata finale. For the moment
this tune makes its leisurely progress, quiet and unassuming,
on strings. Eight bars bring a restatement adding woodwind
and four horns, and, all in a straight line, Ex. 47 appears as a
natural consequence, against a texture of quaver triplets (Ex.
48) – which just happen to feature Ex. 47. The harmony, still

Ex. 48

E flat, becomes minor with this theme, deriving from Ex. 25
and bringing with it a toughening of mood (Ex. 49). It is

Ex. 49

immediately followed by Exx. 45 and 47 building up a climax,
with more and more of the orchestra joining in, to a full
statement of Ex. 49, followed by two bars of it leading straight
on to G major with the same theme. By this time, with no
change in the beat speed, it has become apparent that the
gentle tempo of Ex. 46, as it begins this main part of the
movement, is really quite fast, with the added details, includ-

ing a slow crescendo, that have gradually accrued. Five bars of G major lead the music on to B major, which arrives as a climax, with the opening music of the first movement in strings and woodwind and a derivative of Ex. 25 striding across on trumpets. And with the appearance of this material, a tremendous sense of coming home makes itself felt – not only because of the theme heard. The reality of E flat is tested here even more than it was in the first movement: the key from the beginning of the finale has been E flat, minor at first, with a touch of its relative major, G flat, then E flat again, now swooping through the other two of the three most important harmonies in the first movement – G major and B major. And strangely enough, the arrival at B major settles the reality of E flat major even more than E flat does, when it comes again after ten bars of that first movement material with Ex. 46 on clarinet. Strings pick it up and lead the harmony to D major, where woodwind carry it further to a very calm resting-place on G major.

Here we might halt for a moment to consider what we have been hearing in this finale, and it seems obvious by now that it is no usual sonata form or rondo finale. What we have been hearing is one new theme, one partly new theme, and a review of past events, very excitingly presented. Also, the main key so far, for too long so far as a sonata movement is concerned, has been E flat major; we have had the original subsidiaries of G major and B major briefly (in reverse order to that of the first movement) and now we have come back to G major. We may call it a key, since it has been prepared by its dominant, D minor changing to D major, but it has no suggestion of a dramatically established new key. There *is* drama in this movement, but it is the kind that lives by reflection and is certainly not tonally based. And over all this music is an atmosphere of waiting for something to arrive.

What comes now is an almost immobile passage over a persistent pedal G and marked *Sehr Ruhig*, with apparently a new theme divided between cor anglais and clarinet. Nonetheless, there is something hauntingly familiar about it, and gradually it becomes evident that it is a deeply beautiful variation of Ex. 46. Quiet string triplet support completes the texture. Violins supply a more intense repetition, with increased support, and as it approaches its end Ex. 47 makes itself heard on flute and cor anglais, answered by Ex. 45. At this point the music has almost ceased to move at all. I am reminded a little of a device favoured at times by Hans Pfitzner, of allowing a very energetic beginning to fine down to immobility, and then gradually to regain energy from that point. Two wonderful examples in his work are the Overture to *Käthchen von Heilbronn* and the first movement of his Piano Quintet. The difference between Schmidt's movement and the Pfitzner examples is that this finale does not start with tremendous energy, but it does have enough to make the point when the music arrives at this G major variation, which has overtones of what is often called a pastoral quality in music. More important is that its sound is a particular Schmidt trait and, in fact, points ahead to certain passages in the oratorio, *Das Buch mit Sieben Siegeln*, written in the mid-1930s.

When the repetition has run its course, a soft, chromatic cadence prefaces a gradual rising chromatic passage accompanied by a resuscitation of tempo, leading harmonically away from G and on to a somewhat distorted B minor with Ex. 49. Still increasing speed the music moves on Ex. 47 to an immediately peaceful second inversion D flat major and Ex. 46, on woodwind, horns and strings. This, too, becomes more agitated, with increasing hints of Ex. 25 and of the Hungarian interlocking sound that came at the climax of the exposition in the first movement. This is carried on for about seven bars, arriving at Ex. 25 *fortissimo*; there is more of the Hungarian sound, and Ex. 49 leads to A major and Ex. 46 on strings, with woodwind joining in after two bars, sweeping on through C major and Ex. 45, from which the chromatic harmonies lead to a huge climax with Ex. 49 on the dominant of E flat major. From here Exx. 45 and 47 haunt the horns, string triplets (again suggesting those two figures) build up a climax on the dominant of E flat major, and we arrive at the final stage of this extraordinary finale.

For the second time Schmidt ends a symphony with a chorale. In the finale of the First Symphony the chorale had a function that was neither melodic nor thematic: to apply a sort

Schmidt with his friends, the composer Josef Marx (centre)
and the oboist Alexander Wunderer, around 1925.

of brake to the movement, to hold it steady, where it came at
first roughly halfway through the movement. In the present
movement it is the final climax, and it is very definitely
thematic. I have shown how, as one hears the Symphony, the
variation theme of the second movement grows out of the
initial material of the first movement. The chorale is a huge
summarised version of that variation theme, in five large
clauses – so that the variation theme can be seen as central to
the whole structure of the work, not merely in approximate
position but in importance. Thematically, the first movement
leads to it, the middle movement deals almost exclusively with
it in a variety of ways, and the finale leads from it to this huge
summation.

A second point concerns what happens between each of the
clauses of the chorale, which is exclusively for brass. Each

clause is separated from the next by a spirited reminiscence of Var. VIII from the middle movement, on strings and woodwind. The effect of the whole is very like a preview of the final 'Hallelujah' Chorus in *Das Buch mit Sieben Siegeln*. In the interlude between the fourth and fifth clauses of the chorale we have once more the quotation from the *Intermezzo* from *Notre Dame* that figured in Var. VIII.

A third and final point: what kind of finale have we heard, after all? Certainly not a sonata movement, nor a rondo, nor (apart from the G major episode) variations, that other standby for a Classical finale, where the work did not end with a minuet (or even where it did – witness the variation-minuet with which Haydn sometimes ended a piano sonata). But in the early Classical days, before increase of size began to pose problems, finales were often in the nature of a short coda to the rest of the work. Allowing for the immensely increased scale of the work as a whole, that is what we have here. I remarked earlier, when we arrived at the G major variation of Ex. 46, that we were listening to a reviewing finale; it has continued in that strain. I also stated that there was an air of waiting for something to arrive. That continued, too, until at last the chorale came, which everything had been waiting for. The movement, the shortest of the three, is a huge coda to the rest, and clinches the design of the whole work, which, given its material, is as near perfect as makes no difference.

IV. SYMPHONY NO. 3 IN A MAJOR
(1927–28)

An even larger gap, of fourteen years, intervened between Schmidt's Second and Third Symphonies than that between his First and Second, but there is a difference. The seven-year gap from the completion of *Notre Dame* to the Second Symphony produced no compositions, so far as we know. The gap between Second and Third, on the other hand, in sheer number of compositions, was the most productive period of his career as a composer. 1914 was a good deal occupied with the long-delayed production of *Notre Dame*, first at Dresden, then at Budapest and, in 1915, Berlin, where there were twenty-one repeat performances. Given that the First World War was in progress at the time, the opera had a reasonable success. There had come, too, performance contracts from all over Europe, and a tour of Europe and America was planned, but all this the War prevented. In 1914, too, Schmidt became Professor of Piano at the State Academy of Music in Vienna. It was 1916 before he found himself working again at composition. As with the *Intermezzo* which had preceded *Notre Dame*, so with his second opera, *Fredigundis*. Here, too, he produced an instrumental work, if not before he began to work on the opera, very soon after, interrupting the opera's progress to write it. This work was the *Variations on the King's Fanfares* from the opera and his first work for the organ, the instrument which came to mean so much to him. With this set of variations he surprised his friend, Alexander Wunderer, in December 1916. The work obviously gave him much food for thought, and refused to lie down, for this was only the first (and the only one remaining unperformed) of four versions. A second, the best-known and also for solo organ, came in 1924, and in 1925 a third for wind alone and a final version for wind, timpanum and organ.

From 1916 until 1921, apart from that first version of the organ variations, Schmidt was occupied with *Fredigundis*, which, after many vicissitudes and anxieties for its composer, was at last given a first performance in Berlin on 19 December 1922. It was given again in Vienna on 8 March 1924. Its next complete performance had to wait two decades for a broadcast under Oswald Kabasta, in 1944; and its most recent performances were conducted by Ernst Märzendorfer in September 1979. The opera has never had a fraction of the moderate success accorded *Notre Dame*, and may never have. On its merits as a stage work I cannot comment, nor on those of its predecessor; I have never seen either performed. But the music of *Fredigundis* – that is a different matter. I shall have more to say about that in another volume.

From 1923 to 1926 Schmidt was busy with instrumental music. The first of his two works for piano and orchestra, the *Concertante Variations on a Theme of Beethoven*, a little more than half his total output of organ music (the largest section of his music in number of works), his First String Quartet and the first of his three Piano Quintets. With the exception of the *Four Little Chorale Preludes* of 1926 the organ works are all large-scale. Generally speaking, during this period there was a considerable amount of sorting-out going on in Schmidt's musical personality; it was separating into various strands. One was the path taken by the organ music, a path of rather hard, grim expression. To this there was one notable exception: the *Weihnachtspräludium und Fuge* in A major, composed in 1934, the character of which strayed in the direction of his chamber music. By 1927 there had been two examples of the latter: the A major String Quartet and the G major Piano Quintet. Schmidt was not a composer with a lot of gimmicks to take the place of a recognisable personality, but he did have a very strong personality, of which the first two Symphonies had already shown a good deal. But it had different facets, and after the E flat Symphony these began to appear and separate. It is not that the music that followed (*Fredigundis* apart for the moment) discounts what is displayed in the E major and E flat Symphonies, but rather that there are essences distilled from them, especially from the E flat, and developed separately – so that we seem to see and hear different sides of a very large and complex personality. The firm, four-square aspect that is discernible in the E flat Symphony is also there in the organ music, but often with a rock-hard atmosphere that at times gives the music the sound of being the work of a different man, with a rather grim outlook. And, in a totally different way, this is true of the chamber music. Again, the line is different; there are passages here and there in the E flat Symphony which seem to give rise to the colour and atmosphere of the A major String Quartet and the Quintets, but again the result is almost like that of a different composer; a man with a very sunny, warm nature.

All this was leading up to 1927 and the start of work on the Third Symphony. Again we are faced with a difference that seems almost the result of a cleavage. The Schmidt who wrote the E major and E flat Symphonies in many ways appears to be a different composer from the one that wrote the A major and C major Symphonies. No doubt there were extra-musical reasons to account for the changes, the fluctuations in personality expression during these years: the catastrophe of his unfortunate first marriage, his wife for years in a mental asylum, his second marriage in 1923, the gradual onset of the heart disease which eventually killed him. All these undoubtedly contributed. But, interesting though it is to consider such circumstances, our concern is with the music.

In spite of the predominance of Schmidt's lyrical invention in those first two Symphonies, in spite of the quiet, reflective passages which are more than moments, they are public works, and their composer is a public orator. More than an actor, he is the whole play. But with the Third Symphony one almost has the impression of eavesdropping on a private conversation. It would be easy to say that compared to the first two it is like chamber music and, up to a point, this is true. But the work is still, at the most, symphonic chamber music, and yet seems to me a very private work. It represents a definite change in the direction of Schmidt's symphonic thinking. Somewhere between that curt breaking-off at the end of the E flat Symphony and the beginning of work on the Third a curtain had come down, and another had gone up – on a quite different scene.

Just when one cannot say, but there is one piece of evidence

Geoffrey and Molly Sephton, photographed around 1920.
Molly's real name was Ruth, although she is generally remembered by her nickname.

to show that that new scene was already coming into being at
least four years earlier, in 1923. The 1916 organ variations
show nothing of it, if one can go by their second (1924)
version, and *Fredigundis* shows nothing of it – but that opera
shows little that connects with any other part of Schmidt's
output. But in 1923 Schmidt married for the second time, and
was very happy in that marriage. In 1923, also, he wrote a
short piano piece, *Romanze*, in A major. It has the distinction
of being the only mature piece of piano music he wrote that is
for two hands. Tschulik tells us[1] that it was written in response
to a request for a piece of dance music from Molly Sephton,
the wife of Geoffrey Sephton, who was a friend of Schmidt, a
poet and a teacher of English who had numbered Schmidt

[1] *op. cit.*, pp. 59–60.

among his pupils. His wife wanted a piece for her dance evenings; what she got did not satisfy her, which is not surprising, for whatever else it is it is not dance music. She also said she did not like the piece. Whatever the truth of this may be, the *Romanze* is dedicated 'To Geoffrey Sephton in remembrance 24th 1922'. Schmidt, of course, may simply have switched the dedication from wife to husband because Molly did not like the piece. But that does not explain everything. Sephton was the bride's witness at Schmidt's second wedding. Alfred Jirasek, the brother of Schmidt's second wife, writes, in his introduction to the first edition of the piece: 'The "Romanze" thus must be looked upon as a gesture of thanks towards the highly esteemed friend'. But not for being his bride's witness, surely? And Schmidt remarried on *13* February 192*3*. Nor simply for teaching him English. The *Romanze* commemorates something that happened on the 24th, 1922. But 24th of what? It has been suggested, very plausibly, by the Franz Schmidt Haus in Perchtoldsdorf that the work was intended as a Christmas gift.

Whatever the solution to this little mystery, the piece itself is invaluable for its own content, and for another reason. As a composition it stands alone for its period in Schmidt's life, and its handling of the keyboard, as well as its material, can only make one regret that it did not lead to more extended two-handed solo piano writing in his maturity. It is a self-contained, reflective piece which now and again shows depths from which it quickly draws back, as though at that time Schmidt did not wish to pursue them. But there came a time when he did. In a sense, this short piece of piano music is the hub on which a good deal of Schmidt's later music turned. Two years later the style of the *Romanze* bore fruit, in the A major String Quartet. The following year, 1926, it developed further in the G major Quintet for piano and strings. Without jettisoning a single characteristic that marks the First Symphony, *Notre Dame* and the Second Symphony, Schmidt was changing in personality; developing, transforming, expressing that personality, bringing to it its new attribute of serenity, with no need to strike attitudes or draw attention to himself.

It is often said that the Third Symphony had its origin in

the competition organised in 1928 by the Columbia Graphophone (*sic*) Company to celebrate the centenary of Schubert's death, in which candidates had either to attempt a completion of Schubert's so-called 'Unfinished' Symphony, or submit an original orchestral work in the spirit of Schubert. Schmidt did indeed submit his A major Symphony, and he won the first prize in the Austrian zone (some have considered that he should have won the whole competition, but that went to the Swedish composer, Kurt Atterberg, for his Sixth Symphony).[3] But I find it difficult to believe that Schmidt began the work with the competition in mind, although he may have begun to think of it in this light as the Symphony progressed. To begin to invent and design a work of such proportions directly for the restrictions of a competition becomes a drag on creativity, and as a rule it shows in the finished article. But the A major Symphony shows no such sign. Nothing interferes with its expression of spontaneity. It is true that in 1928, in his Inaugural Address as Dean of the Vienna Academy, Schmidt identified himself very closely with Schubert's manner of musical thought.

First Movement: Allegro Molto Moderato

The first movement opens with the most spirited lyrical outpouring to be found in any of the four first movements. It sings like a lark, with its high-pitched woodwind sound (Ex. 50). Note the rising fourths and thirds. Much drama results from the action of these intervals. What is also interesting is that, whether or not Schmidt was aware of it, while the two tunes are different entities the first four bars of Ex. 50 have exactly the same rhythmic shape as the first four bars of the variation theme from the E flat Symphony (Ex. 33).

[2] Apparently, Max von Shillings, a member of the jury, said that if the winner were not German, no Austrian should win. (Another of the works submitted was Havergal Brian's *Gothic* Symphony, of which only Part I was considered for the competition, Part II including a chorus and therefore being ineligible. Brian was told that the jury, which included Nielsen, Tovey and Glazunov, spent all day deliberating between Atterberg's Sixth and his *Gothic* Symphony before choosing the former, on Glazunov's casting vote.)

Ex. 50

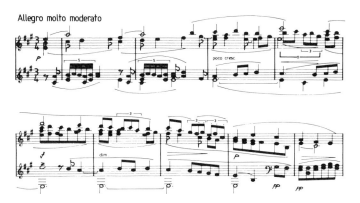

Schmidt's procedure here is a dangerous one. Schubert will often begin a sonata movement with a lyrical idea, but it is short as a rule (there are exceptions, one of them in the same key as Schmidt's Third Symphony), and offset by some other procedure, usually a rhythmical one, which prevents the lyricism from upsetting the apple cart or getting too strong a hold. I cannot recall his ever allowing the lyrical the full rein that Schmidt gives it here, without a safeguard of some sort, however unexpected. The tune of which the beginning is shown in Ex. 50 continues for another five bars, in which the rising third and fourth are prominent, and runs straight into a counterstatement. Counterstatements are usually at the same pitch as the original; the saving grace of Schmidt's is that it is not, but on C major, and only the eight bars shown in Ex. 50 are restated, with some differences of detail in the inner parts.

Those inner parts are another facet of Schmidt's defence against the dramatic aspect of his sonata movement being drowned in lyricism. They are very cunningly contrived, sufficiently contrapuntal to give constant harmonic movement to the music, but not designed in any way to halt or retard the tempo; rather, they tend to push it forward. There is the turn, with Schmidt's personal accent; there is the line just below the tune, moving effortlessly to the fourth bar, where it anticipates the sixth bar of the melody, fig. a, an important figure in the movement in more ways than one.

The five-bar link to the counterstatement is on the dominant, and brings (Ex. 51), another definite Schmidt sound.

Ex. 51

There were traces of this sound here and there in the first two Symphonies, more particularly in the Second, but here it has become a natural part of his whole language. It is a good deal concerned with the augmented triad, another feature which has been used by innumerable composers, each of which has given it his (in the case of Ethel Smyth, her) own accent. Schmidt certainly gave it his. The two bars quoted in Ex. 51 would be enough for anyone conversant with a fair amount of his work but not knowing this Symphony to mark the sound as Schmidt and no one else. The dissonances in the second bar only add to this personal sound.

Already, at the end of the curtailed counterstatement on C major of Ex. 50, fig. a is extending itself and moves into a passage of close descending chromatic thirds and fourths against a rising chromatic bass on cellos (with trills) and bassoon. This is the first of two prophetic passages (Ex. 52),

Ex. 52

looking ahead by five years or so to the Fourth Symphony. It is followed immediately by the second (Ex. 53), a rhythmicly diminished version of Ex. 50. This opens out, through a rising thematic line and descending bass, to a heart-warming climax on the subdominant (with the sixth above at the peak) and a gradual descent to the tonic. And – this climax is strikingly

Ex. 53

similar to one which occurs shortly after the beginning of the piano *Romanze* of four years earlier.

From the beginning of the movement up to this point has been one long outpouring of melody, and it has not finished yet. Schmidt here set himself a bigger problem than Schubert ever faced; Schubert always had a tonal or rhythmic defence (or both) to work for him, so that the lyrical tune was rarely, if ever, put in the position of trying to activate the dramatic aspect of the movement. Apart from the normal tonal scheme of a sonata movement, Schmidt has given himself no such defence. Nonetheless, he solved the problem, in a way we shall see, rather by insisting upon the lyrical than by restraining it.

As the climax comes to rest on the tonic, Ex. 50 is heard again, in the manner of the five-bar link between Ex. 50 and the C major version of that tune. It borrows the rhythmic emphasis of that link, so that what was originally an upbeat becomes the first beat of the bar. Again the augmented triad is heard, again the two bars of Ex. 51 lead, with a logical extension, to a new harmony, that of F minor. The music is leaving A major. A few bars confirm that this is not another harmonic detour which will come eventually back to A, so that the music has definitely left A major, wherever it may be going. With F minor we have a new idea (Ex. 54) – new as it comes to us, but compounded of elements we already know. Fourths and thirds are plentiful and, whether by accident or design, the last five notes of the theme in Ex. 54a are a reversed version of two bars of the passage which led to this new idea, as a comparison with Ex. 54b will show. This could well have been accidental, but it is there and probably only emphasises how strongly Schmidt's mind was moving along this line of thought; but I did hear this reversal in performance long before I saw a copy of the music. The shape of the theme

Ex. 54

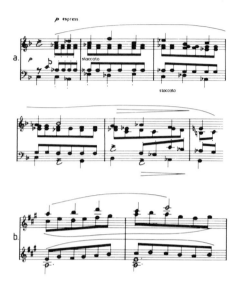

in Ex. 54a is loosely mirrored in the bass, the texture being completed by repeated quaver chords.

So far long pedal notes have been a feature of the bass, and this is another thing which could have militated against any dramatic force being present in the music, but Schmidt has carefully guarded against any clogging of the music's movement, as the constant movement of other parts has made it seem anything but static. Sometimes a bass that remains static for a number of bars (even a large number) and then moves suddenly and quickly is as effective in propelling drama as a bass that is constantly moving, as Edmund Rubbra's Symphonies frequently demonstrate.

Ex. 54a shifts on to C minor harmony. The mirror-like final five notes are extended to finish with a three-note figure (Ex. 55) which, as Ex. 55b shows, is immediately picked up and extended to an interval, B to F, which reminds us, by its rhythm as well as by the fact that it rises, of Ex. 50 and its derivatives. Schmidt is gradually revealing his plan for secur-

Ex. 55

ing the elements of drama in the movement of his lyrical music. Ex. 55b is immediately twice repeated, once from C, again from F, each time with the final note docked, from which the music descends steadily with a chromatic inner part and chromatically rising bass, the upper line containing hints at bits of Ex. 50. The music dies out, suspended in mid-air. The harmony is actually a dominant seventh of F, with a final tenor run up to a D flat, turning the chord to a diminished seventh. The device is reminiscent of similar cases in Reger's music, but sounds like Schmidt.

The main tune (Ex. 56) of the second group is a mine of quite ordinary things, used by innumerable composers in a

Ex. 56

variety of ways, on which Schmidt has managed to put his stamp, so that they sound like him and no one else. First is the diminished seventh in the second bar, against the tonic fifth in the bass. Second is the turn in the fourth bar, on a major seventh, with all Schmidt's personal flavour, and third is the major seventh against the F bass in the fourth bar. One of the most potent things, which shows that much lies beneath the surface of this lyrical tune, is the fact that it has energy enough to make a quite large climax in the fifth bar, which yet does not sound exaggerated. Another of Schmidt's opening out chromatic passages, treble rising, bass descending, leads to a counterstatement and, as with Ex. 50, it is at a different pitch. The counterstatement to Ex. 50, however, was at least on major harmony, which fitted with the original. What adds piquant drama to the present passage is that this counterstatement is on D minor. But it is not so much the minor harmony that disturbs the equilibrium of the music as the fact that it brings with it a number of dark Neapolitan sixth harmonies which stand out from the warmth of the rest, and one of which, on horns, while momentarily intensifying the darkness, actually brings back the light that has for some bars been banished. As the music descends in pitch and volume and arrives at the tonic chord of F major (in a second inversion) it is caught up on a derivative of the beginning of Ex. 50 and rises again rapidly to a climax in which derivatives of Ex. 50, fig. a, are prominent, with a closing section, firmly founded on the tonic, in which the rising and falling fourths are to the fore, with all Schmidt's highly personal chromaticism floating around like incense.

We are switched suddenly back to the beginning for a repetition of this most individual exposition; second time around the music switches just as suddenly from F major to Ex. 50 on F sharp major. I know of few movements in the literature of the symphony or of sonata structure in general, if indeed there is another, in which a fairly lengthy lyrical tune is stated so many times as in this movement – it comes thirteen times. Admittedly, two appearances have it diminished, a few have misplaced accents, and some are inverted – but the inversions are plainly recognisable for what they are. And yet,

The Schmidt residence from 1926: Lohnsteinstrasse 4 in Perchtoldsdorf, now known as the Franz Schmidt Haus.

in some magical way, the movement does not come over as mainly a number of repetitions of the same tune. The repetitions are cumulative, in effect as well as in number, and somehow manage to convey the impression that ground is being covered and drama enacted. A good deal is due to the supporting harmonic counterpoint, which has a constant yet ever-changing flow. F sharp major becomes F sharp minor, with yet another version. The F sharp major version is almost entirely over a dominant pedal, that on F sharp minor also for its opening bars, after which the bass moves widely.

This minor version, or variation, has, in its seventh bar (Ex. 57), because of its minor mode, a harmonic effect made stronger later, which looks ahead to the Fourth Symphony (second bar of Ex. 57). The climax here, on fig. a of Ex. 50, brings the music to C minor and a new stage, with Ex. 50 inverted. Naturally, the minor mode brings opportunity,

Ex. 57

reinforced by the inversion, for new supporting counterpoint. But the most striking aspect of this C minor passage is that it appears as an outcome of what precedes it; it grows out of the past, with a new intensity and offsetting the relaxed nature of much of the exposition. We are hearing a true development.

Another factor in the character of this passage is the nature of the inversion. It is by no means exact; in fact, the intervals at times do not correspond with the original. It is the inverted direction of those intervals and the shape of the inverted melodic line which tell us clearly that we are unmistakably listening to an inverted form, or variation, of that original tune. All these aspects and characteristics coalesce into fine continuing dramatic development, adding to the impact as the music proceeds.

The last few bars of the inversion move with a crescendo through A flat to B minor, utilising the inversion of the opening fourth, then enlarging it (Ex. 58) to a fifth, and on B

Ex. 58

minor Ex. 50, restored to normal, arises on violas, in beautiful two- and three-part string writing. Fig. a of Ex. 50 descends bar by bar to a resumption of the inverted fourth and fifth process, which now takes the music to D minor and a development of those intervals along with fig. a. This leads to a development (Ex. 59) of the upper part of bar 5 of Ex. 50,

Ex. 59

here minor instead of major. Three times the two notes come, B flat and A, separated each time by a bar based on fig. a. Each time the harmony is different: first, second inversion of D minor; second, second inversion of B flat moving to first inversion of D major, F sharp in bass, F natural on top; third, basic dominant seventh chord of G minor, with B flat on top resolving to A.

The increasing tension of these bars, up to the climax in the penultimate bar of Ex. 59, is not only exciting in itself but, with hindsight, prophetic also. It looks, and that penultimate bar especially, forward across five years to the Fourth Symphony. Indeed, there are many signs in this Third Symphony that Schmidt, no doubt unconsciously, was conceiving not one but two symphonies, of which the second came to fruition only in 1933. (Those who know the *Adagio* of the Fourth Symphony can compare the central climactic chord and the progression that follows it, which come roughly midway in the tenebrous middle section of the movement (see Ex. 99 on p. 135), with the penultimate bar of Ex. 59. Obviously, the later example is much more intense, but with an intensity derived from context, the like of which this first movement of the Third Symphony for the most part knows nothing – at least, on the surface.) Yet this lyrical Third Symphony was dropping hints in its progress, hints that would stay with Schmidt and eventually burgeon into the Fourth Symphony.

The climax subsides, on fig. a of Ex. 50, into a passage resembling, but not the same as, Ex. 52, and this leads, through sundry hints of falling fourths and thirds, all over the dominant of A, to the recapitulation. Except that a neat extension of harmony brings the counterstatement on F instead of C major, the recapitulation follows the exposition closely. Ex. 54 now comes on A minor, the second group in A major. Its closing bars now lead to a coda, which begins with Ex. 50 on C sharp major, the brightest harmony on which it has appeared. It builds a climax on the dominant of C sharp, related to Ex. 59, and subsides into a final version of Ex. 50 (Ex. 60).

Ex. 60

But it is Ex. 56 which emphatically ends the movement, with a final reference to Ex. 50, through the five-note turn and a triplet of fig. a, a reference which grows naturally out of the second-group tune – which even more naturally rounds it off.

Second Movement: Adagio

After the beautifully balanced and lyrically structured first movement the *Adagio* came to me initially as something of a shock. I first came to know the Third Symphony through a piano arrangement, only a year or two after I first heard the work played. Whereas the first movement comes off quite well on the piano, though with nothing of the radiance given it by Schmidt's orchestration, the dissonances of the *Adagio*, which had already surprised me to some extent when I first heard the work, do nothing on the piano, with its direct approach (you cannot slide into a sound on the piano), except distort the whole thing. The orchestra makes all the difference in the world. Nonetheless, even with the softening influence of the strings, the sound can still be rather disconcerting. Gradually it does fit into its surroundings, and I know it now as one of the noblest slow movements in my experience.

The movement is possibly the most far-reaching example of Schmidt's highly individual diatonic chromaticism, with a tendency, also, towards what is mistakenly known as bitonality. The fundamental key is never in question – it never is in cases genuinely offered as bitonal. And Schmidt's movement simply is not bitonal.

Harmonically, the piece features a good deal of Schmidt's own individual use of the augmented triad – in fact, it begins with one in the upper strings, with a D minor triad underneath, although Schmidt spells this with an E sharp instead of F (Ex. 61).

Ex. 61

I have noted that the first movement drops hints that were acted upon five years later, in the Fourth Symphony. It almost seems as though this *Adagio* also dropped hints, not for the Fourth Symphony, but for the A major Quintet, which came eleven years later, in 1938. Compare Ex. 61 with the beginning of the *Intermezzo* for solo piano which formed the second movement of the Quintet. (I put it this way because, although the Quintet is played today as a five-movement work with two slow movements, it was written as a four-movement work with one slow movement, the *Intermezzo*. Paul Wittgenstein, for whom the work was composed, wrote that he had doubts about the piece because of its form and feared that quartets

The view from the room in Perchtolds- dorf where Schmidt composed most of his later music. On a good day you can see Pressburg (now Bratislava), where he was born.

would take exception to this movement for solo piano in a chamber work. Eventually he prevailed upon Schmidt to write another slow movement for all five players, intended to replace the *Intermezzo*. But quartets have not objected to the movement for piano solo, and the new slow movement has merely made an additional movement, placed between the scherzo and finale, for which I for one am grateful.)

In shape the *Adagio* of the Third Symphony is loosely a set of variations, actual and suggested. The theme continues for another twelve bars after Ex. 61, starting now from F major, then gives way to an interlude, still in D minor, based on the dip of the melody in the first bar of Ex. 61. After four bars, it begins to follow the theme more closely (Ex. 62). This is the first suggested variation. It leads to the first real variation, on

Ex. 62

Ex. 63

woodwind and brass (Ex. 63). This is in A major, and it is, in
fact, a variation of the twelve bars that followed Ex. 61, which
build a climax. A link of five bars leads to the most impassioned part of the movement, an outburst for strings on E
flat minor, with a theme (Ex. 64) obviously suggested by Ex.
61. As Ex. 64 shows, this swings to E major and on that
harmony we have Ex. 63, diminished to crotchets and quavers

Ex. 64

instead of minims and crotchets, and with yet new contrapuntal support. With a chromatic extension and a surging
crescendo the music arrives at Ex. 64, now on F minor, played
this time by woodwind and horns, trombones and strings.
This time it moves on to F sharp major, with the first
introduction into the movement of a continuous quaver triplet
texture, on second violins and violas. Against them woodwind
play a faint suggestion of Ex. 61, which tails off so that only
one chord is left quietly holding – a chord of C sharp, A sharp,
G natural and E, reading downwards. After a crotchet's

silence Ex. 61 is heard, on strings as originally, with an added quaver triplet counterpoint on clarinet. An interesting point about that held chord is that it resolves to *part* of the opening chord of Ex. 61 – the upper part, the augmented triad of D, B flat, F sharp, again reading downwards. The lower part of the chord, the D minor triad, is added almost casually, to complete the original sound.

Eight bars of Ex. 61 bring the music to Ex. 62 now on A minor and with a persistent oscillating triplet fifth in support from cellos. As before this leads to Ex. 63, now in D major, followed by a coda based on the unquoted four-bar interlude originally leading to Ex. 62. On this, and fragments from it, the movement fades out in D major, the oscillating triplet fifths persisting up to the final chord, transferred in the coda from cellos to second violins and violas.

So we have a sort of variation movement, making a sort of sonata movement, in shape if not in spirit, of which the impassioned E flat minor and F minor passages are the development.

Third Movement: Allegro vivace

Again the Austrian *Ländler* appears to have been the basis of this scherzo. Although by its crotchet movement it is fast, the main theme, in its rhythm, puts such an accent on the first beat of each bar that it seems slower than it is (Ex. 65). The introductory crotchets, on violas and cellos, set against the theme, on woodwind, beginning at the fifth bar of Ex. 65,

Ex. 65

show the two tempi, of which the second predominates. It has, too, a certain relationship in style and mood with the scherzo of the Second Symphony, almost the only point of contact between the two works. Not only does this scherzo cast a look backwards, but also, as a fulcrum between Second Symphony and Second String Quartet, it casts a look forward, for there are many points of resemblance between the present scherzo and that of the G major Quartet, written only shortly afterwards, in 1929. Nonetheless, the present scherzo is a very different movement from either of the others. Even when Schmidt's thinking started from similar premises it always produced quite different results.

The theme continues, starting now from D flat major, and brings a link of eight bars to the theme yet again, this time starting from C major. These are merely transient harmonies; the harmony is moving all the time, but purposefully although chromatically, and now leads to a *legato* theme (Ex. 66)

Ex. 66

starting with a rising third. From here the music makes an almost straight but unhurried move for the dominant of E major, where we have another new theme (Ex. 67), this time

Ex. 67

involving a rising fourth. Here the relationship with the first
movement is plain – Exx. 50 and 57, for instance. The tempo,
though faster in the scherzo, is not so much so as to hide the
resemblance. Ex. 67 acts as a second subject, in a definite E
major, and it is followed by the theme from Ex. 65 making a
coda to the first part.

The second part of the movement begins (Ex. 68) by
turning the crotchet introduction in Ex. 65 into a subject for a
fugato, of which we get three entries before switching to the
main theme on F major, *legato* against a *staccato* bass. The
sharpness of rhythm has gone for the moment, the quaver rest
has gone, and as a result the *Ländler* aspect of the music is

Ex. 68

much more apparent. The harmony lingers awhile around F,
both as tonic of the key and then as dominant of a B flat which
does not really fully materialise, while the bass for a few bars
is *legato*, too. We pass on to the *legato* link that followed the
first four bars of the theme in Ex. 65, the *staccato* bass resumed,
the harmonies moving quickly from bar to bar, eventually
landing on C sharp major, where the *legato* version of Ex. 65
takes over again. Now begins a long crescendo from *piano* over
twelve bars, for eight of which the bass remains C sharp. Then
it begins to move down chromatically, the music arriving at a
climax on a chord of E. And here once more the music looks
ahead across five years to the Fourth Symphony, in a passage
(Ex. 69) which must be heard for the sound to be appreciated.
It brings a momentary suggestion of disruption, but it *is* only
momentary; it manages to hold on to the lighter character of
the music and leads eventually to Ex. 65 for a recapitulation.
Ex. 69 is the one disturbing moment in this exceptionally fine
scherzo. But its disruptive character stayed with Schmidt,
possibly buried deep. At any rate, it surfaced again on a larger
and more catastrophic scale at the end of the development in
the first movement of the Fourth Symphony. When the pieces

Ex. 69

have fallen and the dust has cleared, one fragment is left to carry the music into the *Adagio*.

The recapitulation follows; harmonies are altered to bring Ex. 65, after the *legato* link, on F major where before it was on C major; this brings Ex. 67 in A major. Otherwise it runs as before, with Ex. 65 extended to make a brief coda, which ends, as Schmidt loves to finish, with mounting excitement on one spot and a sudden A major chord, snapped off as it sounds.

The Trio, marked *Molto più tranquillo*, accentuates the *Ländler* character. A link on the notes A and C sharp leads to F sharp major, plunged into rather deviously by means of more 'bitonal' writing in the first chord: a D major triad on top, fifth of F sharp and C sharp beneath (Ex. 70). But it is not only the chord that marks this as peculiarly Schmidt rather than any other composer. In fact, the chord alone would not do it,

Ex. 70			Molto più tranquillo

although it might suggest it. What clinches it is the second chord; only a change from D natural to D sharp on top, and from F sharp to C sharp in the bass, but it is enough. Ex. 70 is a singularly beautiful theme, but, allowing for one thing, other composers might have written it. What, for me, gives it a particular Schmidtian property is the rising of the first two notes of the tune, D natural to D sharp – moving away from the fifth of the F sharp chord before falling to it; and the semitone drop at the end from A sharp to G double sharp. These two facts make all the difference; and the lower harmony has its personal characteristics, too.

As the music continues, there is a gentle rocking motion imparted by the bass and the minim-crotchet rhythm of the tenor part, on the lines already shown in Ex. 70. The first part comes to rest on C sharp major, which is normal enough, once one has absorbed the somewhat unusual way into the key of F sharp major. The first part is repeated.

In the first movement we heard some inverted versions of the main theme that were not exact. The second part of this trio begins with an inexact inversion of the theme from Ex. 70 – but one that is just as recognisable as those in the first movement. It leads to a hesitating passage on a diminished seventh of A flat, F natural, D natural and B, reading down, with a bass hovering round B. This resolves down to Ex. 70 on B major and a much extended restatement of the material of the first part with, whether by accident or design, a passage of rising fourths which recalls the main theme of the first movement (Ex. 50). The bar of crotchets it ends with hesitates twice, the hesitations separated by drumrolls, and then the crotchets become *staccato* and accelerate to repeat the scherzo.

Fourth Movement: Lento – Allegro Vivace

Sir Donald Tovey pointed out[3] that Brahms was not much given to writing introductions; at the moment, I can think of

[3] *Essays in Musical Analysis*, Volume I, *Symphonies 1*, Oxford University Press, London, 1935, p. 85; reprinted in *Symphonies and Other Orchestral Works*, O.U.P., London, 1981.

only four, and the peculiar thing is that three of them are to finales. There is one to the finale of the F sharp minor Piano Sonata, Op. 2, one to the finale of the Piano Quintet, Op. 34, and one each to the first movement and finale of the First Symphony; and the first of these two was an afterthought. There are five in Schmidt's work, and since his total published output is far less than that of Brahms, this makes his proportion of introductions higher. One of his five is to the finale of this Third Symphony. The others are to the first movement of the First Symphony, to the *Variations on a Theme of Beethoven* for piano and orchestra, a brief one to the finale of the A major String Quartet, and one to the *Hussar Variations*.

The present introduction is probably the most beautiful, as it is one of the most beautiful passages in the whole of Schmidt's music. At first sight, it suggests a certain likeness to the introduction to Bruckner's Fifth Symphony: a chorale-like tune and *pizzicato* chords for support. But that is at sight; hearing reveals a totally different conception.

All the woodwind, except bassoons, and two horns in unison begin the chorale tune, breaking after a few bars into harmony, strings gently *pizzicato* making a slow march of the crotchet beats (Ex. 71). Two more bars bring us to D minor

Ex. 71

harmony, where the theme starts again in full harmony, and comes to the beginning of a closing phrase (Ex. 72). From Ex. 72 the theme makes a beautiful cadence, to begin again from

Ex. 72

the tonic on trombones, the *pizzicati* transferred to violins. This time, after four bars, it is deflected to C minor, where a much edited version leads to Ex. 72 again, now resolving on a first inversion chord of D. All this time, volume is gradually increasing, continually being damped and then breaking out again. For the last time the tune of Ex. 71 begins, on D minor, but with a curious change in its beginning (Ex. 73). This, too,

Ex. 73

builds to a *forte*, and brings Ex. 72 for the third and by far the most impressive version (Ex. 74). This full-throated sound, with the arrival at the beautifully placed dominant seventh of C, is pure Schmidt and the highlight of this introduction.

Ex. 74

From here the introduction gradually dies down, fading on a repeated dominant chord of A. Then, at last, the finale proper breaks out, *Allegro Vivace*, with a $\frac{6}{8}$ version of Ex. 71 on strings, and still in A minor (Ex. 75). This continues with the same theme from subdominant harmony, with one difference, and

Ex. 75

Allegro vivace

makes a cadence to the tonic to complete the statement, whereupon it begins again, woodwind added to strings this time. The difference is this: the fourth bar of Ex. 75 is an extension of the third bar. Sometimes, as in this continuation from D minor, that extension is absent. This makes a difference to the sequence of harmonies and, coupled with Schmidt's inherently chromatic style, enables him to move the music in any direction he likes.

This time the subdominant part of the statement retains that fourth bar, and the music is extended through E flat minor before coming at last to the original cadence music, which is much expanded now, and brings us to a new idea (Ex. 76). There are six main ideas, of which Ex. 76 is the second. All six, different as they are from each other, although two are related, are magnificent. Ex. 76 is a transition theme,

Ex. 76

but its accented drum rhythm haunts the music, particularly since the theme itself, as one hears it, appears to grow from that rhythm. As with the main theme there are two beginnings to Ex. 76, the first from A minor, the key of the movement, the second from C minor, a minor third higher. With its octave leaps it moves gradually to the dominant of C and the main theme (Ex. 77) of the second group. This is the third of the six ideas, and utilises the $\frac{6}{8}$ rhythm again in a different way. It is all but diatonic, its chromatic moments, both in the theme

Ex. 77

and in the harmony, few, and this gives it a very different character, calm and confident, from that of either Ex. 75 or Ex. 76. It is a characteristic happy song, bounced along by the bass notes on each half-bar, until we come to what may be called the refrain (Ex. 78), where a melodic figure passes in overlaps from one part to another and a middle part has an echo of the rhythm of Ex. 76.

Ex. 78

Ex. 78 leads to a repeat of Ex. 77 (with one exception, every theme in this movement is immediately repeated, the second time usually with a different harmonic continuation, and fuller orchestration). The repetition of Ex. 78 brings the fourth of the six themes, the closing theme of this exposition and the only one that is not immediately repeated (Ex. 79). It is a thing of light and air, playing on two different versions of the same rhythm, quaver and crotchet, one on the beat, one off. This swings around a harmony of E major, which is maintained for many bars, the rhythm gradually permeated by the repeated quavers that haunt Ex. 76, until the music moves

Ex. 79

into Ex. 75 at its original pitch.

So far as structure is concerned, there has been nothing so far to hint that we are not listening to a sonata movement, but if that is what it is, it is an unusual one, primarily because from its beginning, following the introduction, there has not been the slightest indication of variation of tempo (I have heard conductors make such variation and always it ruins the movement and its effect on the whole work). In fact, there is no indicated variation of tempo at all in the movement and there should be none. A good deal of the happy hypnotic power of this finale is lost if the tempo varies. Contrast here depends upon the differences between themes, the order in which the themes come, the contracting and expanding of rhythms, and the light and shade of Schmidt's dynamics. Add to this the fact that the differences between the themes do not prevent their rolling out in a connected stream.

The development, if that is what it is, continues with the whole of Ex. 75, including the subdominant repetition, then moves on to a further repetition starting on E minor. This time the cadential passage lingers, moving around C, which becomes the dominant of F minor. In this key we have the fifth of the six themes (Ex. 80). So our sonata movement begins to sound like a sonata rondo. There is a sternness about Ex. 80

Ex. 80

A photograph taken
in Perchtoldsdorf in
1937. The illnesses
that were to kill
Schmidt can be seen
in the relative sever-
ity of his appearance.

which deepens and stiffens the character of the movement,
although there is nowhere any hint of tragic drama. Nor is
there any preparation for this theme, no slight holding back,
nothing but the change to minor harmony in the bars
preceding it; and since we have already heard most of those
bars in A minor, there is little that is premonitory about them.
This Symphony does not deal in tragedy, but its finale does
somewhat emphasise the underside of happiness, far more
than the lamenting *Adagio*. This is something which Schmidt
was to explore far more in the years ahead, moving into
terrain of which the Third Symphony has no suspicion.

Ex. 80 is repeated on C minor and comes to a passage on
the dominant of that harmony, repeated quavers prominent in
the bass, from which the music slides into the last of the six
themes (Ex. 81) on E flat major; this has a character
connection with Ex. 77, in fact, it could almost have grown out
of it. As with all but one of the other five themes, this is
immediately repeated, but on G major where the original
bouncy bass is replaced by a sustained dominant of G. A brief
examination of Ex. 81 will give us quite an idea of the kind of

Ex. 81

peculiarities that make Schmidt's theme his own. This one, for instance, avoids the expected B flat on the second note of the second bar, substituting C flat, replacing it with the normal B flat on the way down. This avoidance is retained in the fourth bar, and in the fifth the C flat becomes the springboard to a variation of the first and third bars. In addition, the phrase in the second bar is carried higher in the fourth and highest in the sixth. Numbers of Schmidt's themes will repay this kind of examination, which will help to build an ever more accurate picture of his musical personality.

From this point the development or, more accurately, middle episode is an alternation of Exx. 80 and 81, each at first with its repetition, each time on different harmonies: Ex. 80 on B minor and F sharp minor, Ex. 81 on F sharp major and B flat major, Ex. 80 on A minor only, followed by Ex. 81 on E major, which now fines down to a resumption of Ex. 75 back on A minor. Throughout these continuous alternating statements the orchestration varies considerably.

Now, by elimination of that original fourth bar, Schmidt keeps the harmony at home, albeit changing to A major after a bar or two, preventing it from straying as it did at the beginning of the movement – so that it can stray further, for, where originally it restarted from A minor, it now restarts from F sharp minor and brings with it a whole crop of harmonies, new in this context. Ex. 76, with its drum rhythm and octave leaps, now also comes on F sharp minor and leads eventually to the heart-warming consolation of Ex. 77 (second group tune) in A major. This sings its way through two statements, the second on the subdominant, full-throated and on its top note. And so to the exposition's closing theme, Ex. 79, back on the tonic.

The last few bars of Ex. 79 lead on to D minor and a coda,

starting with Ex. 75, which seems to have gained a new and
rather fiercer lease of life. Once more, although the general
outline is followed, we have harmonic changes, but eventually
the music comes to Ex. 76 *fortissimo*, and it is this theme,
following an *accelerando*, which ends this remarkable movement, the theme being drawn out into syncopated crotchets
(Ex. 82), thus securing the suggestion of a *ritardando* in the

Ex. 82

music without actually writing one. To add one in performance would be (and has been) ruinous. The final chord, the
end of the phrase, is, as is Schmidt's habit with endings, short
and snapped off.

There is still one aspect of this finale which I have not
discussed – the fact that it is in A *minor*, although the
Symphony is basically in A major. Works in minor keys which
have finales in the major reversion of that minor key are
common enough. But the reverse is rare. Brahms' Third
Symphony is one, but that, as with Schmidt's present finale,
turns back to major with the coda. The finale of Mendelssohn's *Italian* Symphony, a work also in A major, is another
instance, and this remains minor to the end. Mendelssohn's
finale is a *saltarello*, and very rapid. Schmidt's Third Symphony finale is a *tarantella*, fast but not so fast as the
Mendelssohn. A much earlier example is the Piano Sonata,
Op. 10, No. 3, by Dussek. This has only two movements, the
first a majestic sonata movement in E major, the second, a
devastating $\frac{6}{8}$ Presto, in E minor and, like Mendelssohn's
Italian finale, it remains minor to the end. A curious case, one
on its own, so far as I know, is the solitary Symphony by the
young Spanish composer, Juan Crisóstomo Arriaga. This

begins with an introduction in D major, passes to a main movement in D minor, and has a finale in D minor which becomes D major towards the end.

Ever since I first knew Schmidt's Third Symphony I have believed it to be in great part an enigmatic work, only to be understood fully (if one can ever fully understand it) in the light of a knowledge of the Fourth. In the last resort the Third Symphony may be the more profound work of the two. It says far more than it shows, whereas the Fourth not only says a lot but shows a good deal of the origin of what it says. There is greatness in the Fourth but no mystery, whereas the Third, great, too, in its own way, is full of mystery, as daylight is more mysterious than its absence.

V. SYMPHONY NO. 4 IN C MAJOR
(1932–33)

The Fourth Symphony was completed in 1933, about six years before Schmidt died, and had its first performance in the following year. It was followed by the E flat Piano Concerto, the oratorio *Das Buch mit Sieben Siegeln*, the last of the three Quintets, a few organ works, including the *Fuga Solemnis*, and the willingly (according to a letter from Schmidt to Franz Schütz) unfinished cantata *Deutsche Auferstehung* – not a large crop in number of works for six years in the life of a composer of Schmidt's stature in the prime of his mental powers. But one of them, the oratorio, is a massive work and itself accounts for two of those years; and there is the fact that the heart disease which eventually killed him was constantly worsening and, through bouts of extreme pain apart from anything else, making it at times impossible for him to work at all.

I have a particular love for the Fourth Symphony, over and above my admiration for it as a work of art, for it was the first work by Schmidt I ever heard performed although not the first work I knew: I already had the printed scores of two of his finest works, the A major String Quartet and the *Chaconne* for organ, both picked up second-hand and very closely studied. This was about 1934 or 1935. In 1936 I found that a two-handed piano arrangement of Schmidt's Fourth Symphony, made by Karl Frotzler, who later also arranged the Third Symphony for two hands, had been issued by Universal. This I bought and almost wore out the copy from playing it so much (not quite, for I still have it and with a bit of repair work occasionally it is quite serviceable). So by the time the Vienna Symphony Orchestra came to London in 1937 I already knew the Fourth very well – except for its orchestral sound, which I could only imagine. The orchestra gave three concerts in Queen's Hall, of which I managed to attend two, and they also did one broadcast – of Schmidt's Fourth Symphony, which was not included in the public concerts.

Oswald Kabasta was their conductor at that time and it was for that orchestra and Kabasta that Schmidt had written the Fourth Symphony. But its composition satisfied, or at least, expressed, a personal need. Musically, leaving aside any extraneous impulse, it was taking up and expanding what had gently started with the Third Symphony five years before; much that was hinted at in that work and even more that lay beneath its surface had simmered and bubbled in his mind, ignoring such effervescences as the Second String Quartet of 1929 and the *Hussar Variations* of 1931 (splendid works both, the Quartet with some surprises, but not concerned in the thread between Third and Fourth Symphonies), until it found the right moment, the right button to press, and pressed it. And in 1932 the Fourth Symphony began to evolve.

There was another spur to his writing this work. Earlier in 1932 his beloved daughter Emma died in child-birth, and in his own words this Symphony was designed as a 'requiem' for her.

First Movement: Allegro Molto Moderato

One thing is immediately new. Nowhere else has Schmidt put the whole of a large work into a nutshell as he does with the 23–bar trumpet tune (Ex. 83) which begins the Fourth Symphony, nor can I think of any similar case from another composer. The designing of this theme is in itself a triumph of compositional skill and genius: it begins at a point a little more than midway between the extremes of the octave of C; it emphasises, under cover of a chromaticism which has the strength usually associated with classical diatonic writing, the two Neapolitan notes of the key of C, D flat and A flat; it insists on fourths as its main interval; these make the overall appeal of this remarkable theme, which makes it easily memorable; it gradually sinks at the end to the tonic it has persistently avoided in anything like a recognisable tonic position; and finally, it alternates between C and D flat, with which it ends – the whole is a masterpiece of symphonic thinking. It is that concluding alternation which pushes the symphony on its way.

Ex. 83

The first result is that C, which we have at last touched as
an unmistakable tonic (it has twice appeared previously, as
Ex. 83 will show, but each time without a tonic sense), moves
up to D flat, which obviously leans on C, the D flat falls back
to C, which this time has already lost some of its tonic quality
and as it moves back to D flat has a definite leading-note
sound about it. At this point, too, we leave the single line and
direct harmony enters. Tschulik has written[1] of Ex. 83 that it
is 'a genuine "lyrical" air, in which the key of the Symphony is
not immediately apparent'. To understand the first part of
that sentence I should have to know what Tschulik means by
'lyrical', and why he finds it necessary to put the word in
inverted commas. But I agree with the second part of his
sentence: C is *not* immediately apparent. It begins to become
so a little more than halfway through the theme, with the rise
from D to G in bars 13 and 14; and from there C becomes
more and more obvious, only to be dissipated, as I have
described, in the bar or two that ends it.

Now, Schmidt has obviously chosen to begin the Symphony
at that tonally indeterminate point, to let the work slide in as if
already in progress. What follows Ex. 83 proves this. The final
C having moved back to D flat, this now remains the basic
harmony for many bars, D flat gently booming in the bass,
and we have Ex. 83 again, fully harmonised this time. But in
front of it (Ex. 84) Schmidt inserts four bars to lead the music
from this resolving D flat to the theme as it starts in Ex. 83.
The extra bars remove any idea that D flat is indeterminate,

[1] *op. cit.*, p. 98.

Ex. 84

as C was to begin with. Leaving aside the D flats in the bass of this counterstatement, Schmidt could have avoided that impression, if he had wished, with regard to C major, even without the added harmony and the bass. But he was right not to: the indeterminate nature of that beginning, unharmonised, sets the scene and the mood for the whole work.

The tempo, too, adds to the impression. *Allegro molto moderato* is Schmidt's direction, but with more accent on *molto moderato* than on *Allegro*. It is not slow but neither is it fast; it moves, steadily, inexorably. It should not be allowed to drag, as unfortunately it sometimes is, for this spoils Schmidt's carefully thought-out shape.

One final point about Ex. 83: in the analysis of the second movement of the Second Symphony I have drawn attention to Schmidt's way of lengthening or shortening the final notes of phrases. He does so here, too, with great effect, sometimes lengthening the sound, sometimes merely adding a rest.

The chromaticism, rooted by the persistent bass D flats to that basic harmony, is naturally increased by the harmonisation of Ex. 83. Again we have the drop of a fifth at the end of the theme, A flat to D flat this time, the move up to D natural, back to D flat, written as C sharp. This time the final chromatic move does not come; instead, C sharp proves to be the dominant of a local F sharp minor harmony, which, however, lasts for only two bars, including the C sharp preparation.

As we shall find, the alternation of the final notes of Ex. 83 proves to be one of the most fruitful ideas in the entire Symphony; nearly always it is responsible for a different direction being taken. Here, having led this time to a momentary (but very solid) F sharp minor, the music begins just as steadily to move upwards chromatically (Ex. 85), with a bass

Ex. 85

moving downwards locally with each phrase, but overall moving up with the upper parts. There are at least two precedents for this steady progression. One is the passage formed of Ex. 53 and the climax which followed from the first movement of the Third Symphony – one of the ways in which that work looks forward to this one. The other is from the first movement of the Second Symphony, Ex. 26. Neither passage has the same effect in its place as Ex. 85; Ex. 53 and its following climax are closer, simply because the language of the movement they come from is much closer to that of the Fourth Symphony. But both show a trend in Schmidt's thinking which had various previous appearances, including the two I have quoted, and which needed to find its most mature and deepest expression. It found it in Ex. 85, where every bit of musical thought is part of one great curve, continuous and moving on at the same steady tempo to its appointed climax, which is built on the first five notes of Ex. 83, the first four as crotchets, the last a minim; and in its own good measured time this arrives at a full-blooded chord of C. No more definite or emphatic assertion of a tonic could be imagined, and as one hears it everything that has happened since the Symphony began, especially its initial avoidance of the tonic, slips into place. So that the movement, from the first trumpet note up to the *fortissimo* chord of C at the peak of the climax, is a gradual finding of the true tonal centre of the work.

The *fortissimo* C major chord is not only a catharsis but at the same time releases more pent-up chromatic gropings from its solid vantage point. Three trumpets move down in whole-bar chords of two perfect fourths pressed together, and against them an oboe sounds a falling figure of quavers also made of descending fourths. After two descents this figure begins to rise, and so does the bass, slowly but inevitably, until the music comes to the dominant of F sharp major; Schmidt gives it that key-signature, but the music that follows is so chromatic that it is difficult to hear in it a major mode. The upper theme is a variation of the first four bars of Ex. 83 and the inner parts are still derived from the harmonised version of that theme, with a C sharp *tremolando* bass. Slowly the music descends, eventually dying out on a quiet chord, left suspended. When discussing (p. 97) the approach to the second group in the first movement of the Third Symphony, I remarked on the likeness to certain procedures of Reger in the way the music arrived at the very last moment at a diminished seventh chord, although it does not sound like Reger. Here we have a similar incident. Again the music is left suspended, again there is a silence, and then the second group's main theme is heard.

The chord on which the music dies out (Ex. 86) is far from haphazard: with the drum's C sharp in the bass, it is a highly

Ex. 86

chromatic *suggestion* of a dominant chord. The G double sharp, after a silence of two beats, resolves up to A sharp for the first

Ex. 87

note of the second group main theme (Ex. 87), which now
breaks out, *Passionato*, on violins. Ex. 87 is the four-bar first
phrase of a two-phrase theme; the second, which repeats and
develops at a different level the material of the first, occupies
six bars because of the climactic repetition of the first bar of
Ex. 87 (not at the same pitch as in that example) and an extra
final note. The pith is in Ex. 87 – a short theme against the 23
bars of Ex. 83.

There are other points to be noted about this theme, the
first being the subdued passion of its beginning. But although
it is marked 'passionate', it is also marked *piano*, a fact noted in
only two performances I have heard: the 1937 broadcast
already referred to, and a wonderful recording by the Vienna
Symphony Orchestra conducted by Rudolf Moralt, made in
the mid-1950s.

A further point is the nature of the tonality of Ex. 87. It
begins solidly in F sharp major and after four crotchets (a
single line making its own harmony) it becomes just as solidly
F sharp minor. Music beginning in the major and becoming
minor, or the reverse, even within the same tune, is not
uncommon. In Schubert it happens frequently. But such a
change within the same phrase, and when that phrase has
barely begun, is so unusual that I can think of only two other
instances that are like it, and one that is similar on the surface,
but not quite the same in effect. Both the first two are by
Dussek. One is the phrase beginning the development in the
finale of his C major Piano Sonata, Op. 9, No. 2. The other is
part of the restatement of the second subject tune in the
recapitulation of the first movement of his Piano Concerto in
G minor, Op. 49. But there is one important difference
between the Schmidt and Dussek: neither of the two Dussek

examples occurs in the first appearance of the theme concerned; the Schmidt does, so that the change from major to
minor is built into its nature from the start. The same
difference also occurs in the third instance. This is the
recapitulated second group main theme in the first movement
of Beethoven's Ninth Symphony. But there is a greater
difference involved here, for the change to minor occurs only
after a complete phrase has been stated in the major. The
whole conception is different, although it involves an applica-
tion of the same principle.

The continuation of Ex. 87, begun by an answering phrase
with its climbing repetition, brings the music to A major,
so-called relative major of F sharp minor. From here the
whole of the two phrases comes again, ending on C major,
letting fall at the end an important quaver figure (Ex. 88). As

Ex. 88

this shows, the quavers land on a derivation from Ex. 87,
which drifts back on to the dominant of F sharp major, and a
figure utilising the quavers builds up a climax (Ex. 89) with a
characteristic Schmidt figure of triplets – one may remember
the triplet figures in the first movement of the Third Symphony. Ex. 89 shows the music tailing off into a figure derived
from the initial crotchets of Ex. 87, marked fig. a. It also shows
the triplets, another form of Schmidt turn which really looks
right back to the *Intermezzo* from *Notre Dame*, and the succeed-
ing bar with its equally characteristic chromaticism.

Fig. a of Ex. 89 continues to drift, over a pedal F sharp, the
harmony descending chromatically, until one begins to get the
impression that the exposition is over and we are moving into
the development. The drift continues, the basic harmony
becoming that of D major, the bass shifting to D, and the
impression of development is momentarily strengthened when

Ex. 89

we hear the first four notes of Ex. 83, diminished in value, reminding us of the treatment accorded Ex. 50 in Ex. 53. The impression is even stronger when, after four bars of this diminished idea, the music sweeps on to Ex. 83, picking it up at its original tenth bar, with a quaver accompaniment that gives it a tremendous sense of movement. It goes as far as the original rise to top G (new top A), then continues with new counterpoint (Ex. 90) over it, including a full bar turn, and

Ex. 90

descending crotchets, the upper counterpoint continuing with a compressed version of the whole bar turn and a surprising figure of crotchets which make an important item, marked fig. b in Ex. 91.

Ex. 91

The final oscillating notes of Ex. 83 are omitted. Instead, Schmidt proceeds to show us that what we have been hearing is not a development but is still expository, at the same time revealing more of the all-embracing depth of Ex. 83. This now sweeps from D major back to F sharp with Ex. 87, a far more passionate statement than the original, not now subdued but full-blooded, and with a rising crotchet counterpoint against the second and third bars, buried in the middle of the harmony, so that it is not too noticeable. There is only one statement of the two phrases this time, and no extra beat's rest between them. They are joined, by means of the quavers we met in Ex. 88, to the climax of Ex. 89, far stronger this time, and leading, again through the quavers, marked *rit.*, to the final passage in this exposition, a *Più Tranquillo* fourteen bars long. Over an F sharp pedal two lines of thirds, thematically made of the triplets from Ex. 89 and the quavers from Ex. 88, push and jostle their chromatic way gradually downward until they come to the initial descending fourth of the movement, here on F sharp and C sharp, with crotchets moving below. This is repeated, passing to F sharp minor, on a horn, whereupon the cor anglais takes it over, down a semitone, and, again a semitone lower still, starting from E, begins Ex. 83. The F sharp pedal is still gently rumbling, and other support comes from quiet *pizzicato* chords. We are in the development.

The scoring throughout is a masterpiece of evocative sound. One of the most imaginative moments in the whole Symphony is in the passage we have just heard, the horn playing the two opening notes of Ex. 83, so that it seems that it is going to play the whole tune, only to be cancelled out immediately by the cor anglais carrying on the musical thought, the horn pushed aside, almost with a sense of contradiction with the lowering of the pitch, and, quiet thought the music is, with a feeling of tension hanging over it.

What has begun with the development is a sort of passacaglia, with Ex. 83 as its basic theme; this occupies roughly half of a quite large development. The cor anglais statement, invoking above it derivatives of the turn and crotchet idea of Ex. 90, moves on through D major to A major, where another

statement comes in the bass, with yet another new figure
above, and with the sensation of emerging from turbulence to
calm. It is not difficult to see that all these 'new' ideas and
figures derive in some way partly from Ex. 83; but they also
derive partly from their immediate surroundings, or are
thrown up by them; hence their completely logical sound.

   The end of this bass statement has a still more compressed
version of the turn and the crotchets of Ex. 91, giving off yet
another theme (Ex. 92). The new theme continues to develop,

Ex. 92

and the final oscillating notes of the bass theme also, so that
the harmony is constantly changing, rising gradually, the
intervals of the bass becoming shorter, moving the music on
and upward inexorably. Moving through the flux of counterpoint can be heard snatches of Ex. 83, at first on horns, then
gradually bits of it permeate the texture, until at last the music
reaches a climax on a resounding first inversion chord of B
major, sharply cut off, so that it echoes in the silence that
follows, filling the remaining two-and-a-half beats of the bar.
The next bar brings the beginning of Ex. 87.

   And now Schmidt brings off a master stroke of developmen-
tal thinking, so that a number of ideas are brought together to
become one entity. Referring back to the full-blooded statement of Ex. 87 in the exposition, there was with it a rising line
of crotchets buried in the middle of the harmony. The first
phrase of Ex. 87 now comes on woodwind, with the rising
crotchets soaring above it on violins, leading up to the final
oscillating notes of Ex. 83, now C sharp and D natural,
harmonised in F sharp major, the final D heralding a move on
to that harmony, with a syncopated tail, and all in a single
thematic phrase (Ex. 93). The dominant seventh shown at the

Ex. 93

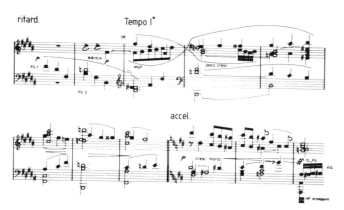

end of Ex. 93 lasts, with woodwind chromatic runs and harp
arpeggios, for four bars, although the pedal A lasts for much
longer. At the end of the fourth bar appears a diminished
version, in quavers, of the tenth and eleventh bars of Ex. 83,
which figure then, with echoes underneath, gradually descends chromatically, with a *molto ritardando*, to the theme
shown in the last four bars of Ex. 92, now marked *Lento*. This
has the oscillating final notes of Ex. 83 beneath it, passes to
the bass and D minor, the oscillating notes above now
gradually beginning to move the harmony chromatically in
the manner of Ex. 85. I have already quoted two precedents
for this type of passage, one from the Second Symphony, the
other from the Third. Something similar happens here, the
bass being formed mainly of the theme from Ex. 92. When the
upper part reaches a top G and the bass a bottom D, the
upper harmony descends chromatically and the bass ascends,
also chromatically, to B flat and a passionate outburst of Ex.
87. This expanding and contracting of the harmony gives the
music a suggestion of breathing.

Two things have happened to this theme since we first
heard it: the rising crotchet counterpoint has become a
permanency and the oscillating notes from the end of Ex. 83
have attached themselves as a tail to the theme. This has a
bearing, too, on the third movement of the work, the scherzo.
In the first phrase of this latest statement the rising crotchets

are again in the middle, but in the second phrase they are on
top (Ex. 94). Ex. 94 moves on to E major with the syncopated

Ex. 94

tail from Ex. 93, which now moves the music rather quickly on
to Ex. 87 again as we have just had it, crotchet counterpoint
on top, and it is immediately repeated, without a break, so
that the two statements seem like a single phrase, moving
back into B flat major.

As may have been noticed, I make a clear distinction
between music moving *on* to a harmony, which means that
that harmony is transient and is not a key, and *into* a fully
established key. Here the music has definitely moved into B
flat major, and this key stays now for quite a long time,
allowing for chromaticisms which do not affect the key, except
to affirm it. As with Ex. 94 this last statement of Ex. 87 has the
syncopated tail from Ex. 93, and now this is used for some
bars, ever a dominant seventh of B flat major, with swirling
harp arpeggios, and comes at last to the passage (Ex. 95) I

Ex. 95

mentioned in dealing with the scherzo of the Third Symphony. Woodwind, trumpets and strings make this shrill and give it the effect of an explosion in which bits of themes fly apart. In fact, what is thematically concerned is the two parts of the phrase contained in Ex. 87 combined, but the harmony, the scoring and the rhythm give it this great explosive effect, so that one can almost *see* bits of themes hurled into the air and descending again. What helps this effect greatly, so that although the two bits of theme are combined they seem to be blown apart, is the cross-accented note that comes halfway through each bar, mainly on clarinets (including an E flat clarinet).

Gradually, the figure of the second bar of Ex. 87 sinks lower and lower, over repeated bass F's. Violas make an attempt at the beginning of Ex. 87, and dissonance cuts them off. More boldly, a solo cello makes the same attempt and with a less dissonant, almost sympathetic, version of the same chord the cello moves into the *Adagio*.

Second Movement: Adagio

This appears to be the one part of the Symphony which has no thematic connection with Ex. 83, other than the fact that the opening cello tune, which dominates all the first and also the final part of the movement, is based on the descending interval of a fourth.

B flat, major at the beginning and the end, is very firmly and unequivocally the tonality of this *Adagio*, with its relative minor, G minor, in the middle part. The movement begins with a solo cello playing one of the loveliest melodies ever conceived (Ex. 96). A full statement by the cello is followed by a counterstatement by orchestral violins, in which, after a detour through C sharp minor, the closing portion of Ex. 96, with the semiquaver sextolet, is expanded to bring the music to E flat harmony for a short development of the beginning of the tune, bringing it to a second inversion B flat major chord for the coda of this huge idea. Here (Ex. 97) the initial interval of a fourth is inverted and the music descends, instead of

Ex. 96

Ex. 97

tending to rise, as it has hitherto in spite of falling intervals.
The bass moves almost throughout in steady slow crotchets,
giving the whole sound of the music a sense of stability which
nothing can disturb. An oboe imparts a singular sweetness to
the last two bars, as the music comes to its final tonic chord,
which, with the introduction of short muffled drum rolls,
reinforced by low strings, moves slowly to G minor and the
middle part of the movement, marked *Più Lento*, the heart of
the whole Symphony.

Even allowing for the immediate repetition of the first eight
bars, the tune which dominates the first part of this movement

is one of the largest ever written, lasting as it does in constant expansion for 26 slow four-crotchet bars – yet there is not a note too many.

The solo cello also initiates (Ex. 98) the mourning music of this central part. The muffled rolls continue almost throughout this section, at first on low woodwind, drum and doublebass, later on bassoons and horns, finally on trombones.

Ex. 98

Ex. 98 contains roughly half of the material, the other half being the funeral dirge that answers the cello theme, taking the music to C sharp minor harmony, where Ex. 98 begins again and, for a time minus the muffled rolls, brings about the largest climax in the movement, of which the beginning (Ex. 99) is the version of the dirge already mentioned in connection with part of the first movement of the Third Symphony. The tenebrous sound of all this middle section, with the intensity of the dirge, is Schmidt's outpouring of grief for the passing, earlier in the year, of his beloved daughter Emma.

Ex. 99

As this huge climactic passage, perhaps the greatest lament in twentieth-century music, sinks to its close, Ex. 98 is resumed on trumpet and violins, with the muffled rolls now on trombones and drum, again in G minor, with, as it were, a reversed climax; that is to say, the harmony is deflected downwards, so that the climbing figure that previously built up the climax here seems to soothe the music, so that if the cause of the grief is still there, there is at least a promise of approaching calm. The muffled rolls continue throughout, becoming softer as the music proceeds. As this statement finishes, Ex. 98 comes yet again, this time on a horn, which gives it a very hollow sound. The final chord moves out to one of E flat minor and a cadence on trombones which is expressively blunted before being carried down to the depths. The sound of this cadence brings to mind some of the quiet, low-pitched trombone writing that came later in *Das Buch mit Sieben Siegeln.*

The skill of the writing throughout this entire middle section, the balancing of phrases, the subtle and, at times, the unleashed yet controlled fullness of volume of the mass of instruments, in which the entire orchestra is shaken by and unified to the expression of the great and noble grief, as unconscious of listeners as are the late String Quartets of Beethoven, is near-miraculous. This section was written not long after the cause of its emotion, the death of Schmidt's daughter, when he was still gripped by the near-despairing grief this event occasioned in him; but somehow he managed to control what shook him to a masterly piece of composition which could easily have lost control and wrecked the work, but which did not. Remembering, too, that he was also wracked by bouts of intense pain, one can have nothing but admiration for the fortitude which held him on his course.

From the quiet connecting drum rolls emerges the solo cello on a low D, moving in an upward arpeggio, initiated by bassoons, in two bars which gradually restore the original *Adagio* tempo and the tune of the first part of the movement on flute, clarinet and bassoon, with a flowing semiquaver counterpoint on second violins and violas, and *pizzicato* chords on the second half of each beat, to which horns are added as the music detours through C sharp minor.

At the end the solo cello has the last word, descending to the depths and rising to the final chord, leading to three quiet drum rolls on B flat, and so into the scherzo.

Early (1906) and later (1922) photographs of Schmidt's
daughter Emma (1902–1932) whose death in childbirth directly
inspired the elegiac mood of the *Adagio* of the Fourth Symphony.

Third Movement: Molto Vivace

The scherzo, a rapid $^6_8$ in B flat minor, starts with a new theme
(Ex. 100) which again uses the descending fourth and pre-
tends, at first, to initiate a fugue. It *is* pretence, however, and
although counterpoint rarely ceases throughout the movement, the music has no intention of saddling itself with the
obligations which go with fugal writing.

Ex. 100

Molto vivace

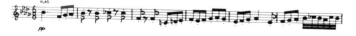

In the three previous Symphonies Schmidt wrote scherzi which, although different in character from each other and blending with their surroundings, share a decided leaning towards the Austrian *Ländler*. There are other scherzi in his work which have the same tendency: those in the two String Quartets, for instance, the one in the B flat Quintet for clarinet, piano and strings, and the trio (but not the scherzo) of the A major Quintet for the same combination. But this one avoids any such suggestion, although we may notice that, in spite of the rapid pace of the music and the $\frac{6}{8}$ rhythm, he does manage to infuse at times a leisurely spirit into the music, as when its initial interval of a fourth causes a dim memory to stir and strengthen, so that very soon we hear Ex. 83 sailing in on top of the music (Ex. 101). This tails off with a derivative of

Ex. 101

Ex. 83 turned into quavers, and Ex. 100 reappears with new scoring and rhythmic presentation, still on B flat minor. This time it moves further afield, through C sharp minor, and Ex. 101 follows, now on A flat major. The tailing-off process leads now to a new theme (Ex. 102), in C sharp minor, derived from Ex. 100, the quaver phrases successively larger. Each half bar

Ex. 102

is marked by heavy chords, as though an army were on the tramp. The answer is the inversion of Ex. 102, the quaver phrases descending. Again Ex. 101 begins to appear, but only the first two bars, which expand to a thematic fragment again related to Ex. 100, which lasts for sixteen bars over a G sharp pedal. Again a change to A flat, this time a momentary dominant of D flat major, and the beginning of Ex. 102 leads to what could be called the trio, in effect and character, although the basic rhythm and tempo do not change, nor does the energy abate (Ex. 103). What matters here is that Ex. 103

Ex. 103

brings an element of contrast and, still more important, that it is the beginning of the second subject theme of the first movement (Ex. 87) treated with the rising counterpoint and the oscillating notes from Ex. 83, as it was in Exx. 93 and 94, but adapted to the $\frac{6}{8}$ rhythm. Harmonic shifts follow each other quickly. Ex. 103 is repeated a third higher, on B major, whereupon the initial bars of Ex. 101 provide an interlude, leading to Ex. 103 again, on G major followed by B flat; this lands on a dominant seventh of A flat which does not resolve but moves to a dominant seventh of F sharp. However, harmony is sliding away all the time here, but from the first two bars of Ex. 103 we gradually find the interval of a fourth slipping back into a suggestion of Ex. 100, and again a gradual tailing off, over the dominant of F sharp, to Ex. 100 fully stated on F sharp, the tramping half-bar chords of Ex. 102 now supporting this theme.

There are no more themes or derivatives to come. What we have had alternate, in a sense dance around each other, a sort of dance of despair, with Ex. 83 or its spirit never far away. Eventually Ex. 103 comes again, with an expansion of several

bars taking the place of the oscillating chords, and bringing a
bar of ⁹₈ to expand further the rhythm, a bar that has a
marvellous consequence later. At last we come to Ex. 100 on
D minor, in a determined effort to realise the fugue that has so
far been abortive. But, in spite of its determined sound, it has
no more luck than before. What it does do is to lead to the
consequence (Ex. 104) of that ⁹₈ bar, with the wonderful

Ex. 104

piercing of the texture by the three trumpet notes, an obvious
yet unexpected reference to part of Ex. 83. Ex. 83 follows.
From here the music is all pitched round F minor. Ex. 83 leads
into Ex. 102, followed by the first two bars of Ex. 101 and its
follow-up with part of Ex. 100, all building up, through a full
statement of Ex. 100 and the beginning of Ex. 102 extended
gradually up the scale and punctuated by chords, to the
climax of this movement, in which, at a much slower tempo,
whole- and half-bar chords descend chromatically and bring
to the foreground (Ex. 105) the grief of the *Adagio*, which has
been so determinedly suppressed throughout this savagely
twisted scherzo. In fact, much of this movement betrays a
fierce bitterness, far removed from the heart-heavy mourning
of the *Adagio*, but springing from the same source.

Ex. 105

Down into the depths the music goes, to a low D flat triad
on trombones, bass tuba descending chromatically below

When the weather was fine, Schmidt took an especial delight in composing in the pavilion at the bottom of his garden in Perchtoldsdorf.

them, double-bassoon on its lowest F, and a very quiet drum roll completing the sound. Everything but the quietly muffled drum roll ceases and, but for that roll, which is, or should be, only just audible, there is a silence that is almost the most eloquent thing in the work, and one of the most awesome moments in symphonic music. This whole passage again reminds one of parts of the later oratorio. It brings up a feeling of hushed awe, which at the same time can make one feel breathless.

So far we have had a work which has been mistakenly called a one-movement symphony, but which is, in fact, a three-movement work. We have had the first movement up to the end of the development (as it proves), which was then side-tracked into the *Adagio*, which itself led, through the connecting drum rolls, to the scherzo. This has now died out, except for the intense quiet of the murmuring continuing drum, and we are about to find out what comes out of these depths. (I have often wondered whether, in writing this astonishing passage, Schmidt ever thought of the words of the

In February 1935, to commemorate Schmidt's sixtieth birthday the previous December, a concert was organised in which the composer conducted the Vienna Philharmonic in the *Variations on a Hussar Theme*, the Piano Concerto in E flat major (the soloist was Ludwig Wittgenstein, who had commissioned it) and the Fourth Symphony (Schmidt's performance of which, at 39 minutes, was around ten minutes faster than Zubin Mehta's with the same orchestra in 1972, to date the only commercial recording (Decca SXL 6544), and seven minutes faster than his own initial estimate, published in the piano score). These photographs were taken at the rehearsal, and that on the bottom right, where Schmidt is shaking hands with Arnold Rosé (whose opinion of the Fourth Symphony was very high indeed), would seem to indicate a degree of cordiality between the two men that, according to Schmidt's *Autobiographical Sketch* (pp. 176–180), was earlier lacking in their relationship.

psalmist: 'Out of the depths have I cried to Thee'.) What does come is one of the miracles of music. Over the still persisting drum roll the first horn very quietly begins Ex. 83 in F, and continues with it up to bar 14, the original top G, here a C, when the third horn joins in, the first horn repeats the G and C, holds the latter and the third horn completes the theme, down to the three oscillating notes. Gradually the other two horns join in and this remarkable theme expands in some of the most wonderful four-horn counterpoint ever conceived, eventually coming to a cadence on F, quietly echoing the big cadence on C to which the opening of the Symphony led. At this point the original repeated bass notes begin on cellos, and the music proceeds from there in a recapitulation. I cannot think of a more astounding reconception of a passage, in any work known to me, or one more governed by the whole action of that part of the Symphony (the larger part) which precedes it. The whole is instinct with genius fully realised and completely controlled, imagination allowed so far and no further.

From the descending chords for three trumpets, as we had them after the first big climax on C, the music follows exactly as before, pitched over F instead of C, so that the long chromatic passage of dominant preparation, with its melodic line derived from Ex. 83, is now on F sharp, leading to B major for the second group. This, too, is recapitulated exactly, until we come to the final passage of the exposition, now of course on B; but instead of moving into the development, as it did previously, it proceeds to a coda which utilises at first the opening of Ex. 83 without continuing with the rest of it. B major changes to B minor, but from there the harmony is chromatically rising all the time. For a moment we get the impression that we are to have the chromatic passage shown in Ex. 85, but this is forestalled and delayed for a few bars, while the harmony mounts higher and eventually creeps into Ex. 85, which builds up to the climactic passage omitted at the beginning of the recapitulation. This originally led to the first big climax on C; here it almost does, but Schmidt achieves an even more impressive effect by turning it aside at the last moment with the chord marked *x* in Ex. 106, which unex-

Ex. 106

pectedly gives the whole work a sudden thrust that is over-whelming. This passage continues to descend and finds itself giving way to Ex. 87 on F–F minor, which continues to drift harmonically and heart-warmingly, with a mounting sense of coming home, in a *ritardando* until, many bars later, it comes at last to C. On the way Ex. 87 has managed to infuse into its harmony a touch of Schmidt's Hungarian gypsy, much as the final bars of Sibelius's Seventh Symphony trespass for a moment on the *Valse Triste* of years earlier.

Even when the music, in the simplest terms, arrives at C, it is not a clear tonic harmony. It has an A flat above it on a horn, which just manages to resolve to G before it is contra-dicted by an A natural on a trumpet, from which, supported by chords of C with mild complications (for a moment not unlike the ending of Mahler's *Das Lied von der Erde*) the trumpet plays the whole of Ex. 83, extending the penultimate D flat into silence. The final C is unsupported, giving the work the satisfied completeness of the proof to a geometrical theorem.

It is interesting that the keys of the first and second subjects, in the recapitulation, are F and B, each a fourth higher than its original, so stressing the importance of the interval of a fourth in the work. It could be accidental, but I doubt if anything in this amazing work is accidental.

It has been said that with the ultimate restatement of Ex. 83 on the trumpet the Symphony has come full circle. It has not. This work is not a serpent with its tail in its mouth. In fact, it is impossible for any music to be circular, for, whatever the beginning and the end may be, something has happened in between which will affect the sound of that ending. We have been on a journey and we have come home, with a depth of understanding we did not have when we set out. And, of course, starting with the beginning of the First Symphony, we have been on an even larger and longer journey. Starting with that E major Symphony, with its individual treatment of late nineteenth-century German feeling, the four works gradually move in reality into the twentieth century. They do not partake of the twelve-note revelation of Schoenberg, although there are times when Schmidt writes twelve-note music of his own, obeying his own rules. They do not share the frenzied, semi-suicidal, live-for-today sentiments that infected so much post-1918 music. They are not programme music, in the normal meaning of that term. They have no part in the avant-garde movement. For those with limited musical outlook this will condemn them. And yet, beginning with certain aspects of the Second Symphony, they are a genuinely twentieth-century phenomenon; and it is certain that neither the Third nor, especially, the Fourth could have been written even in the late nineteenth century, the period of the First. That Schmidt is one of the greatest and most independent of symphonists cannot, I think, with reason, be denied, nor that, even if the First misses the masterpiece class, his other three examples will stand as masterpieces for a very long time. It will prove very difficult to surpass them.

VI. CHACONNE IN C SHARP MINOR
(1925, orchestrated 1931)

A brief word about Schmidt's other orchestral works. There are only two for orchestra alone: the orchestral version of his organ *Chaconne* and the *Variations on a Hussar Song*. Both were completed in 1931; the organ *Chaconne* in 1925. The case of the *Chaconne* brings up some interesting points, not least as to the status of his organ music in general.

First is the question of transferring a whole work from one medium, for which it was originally conceived, to another. This is a practice which can be found in the Baroque period, when media were not so clearly defined and fenced off from each other, and especially in Bach's work; but he almost always recomposed the original for the new medium. And from Classical times onwards even this practice has almost died out (there are some exceptions). Mozart transcribed the C minor Fugue from a two-piano original, K.426, for string quartet, with certain differences, and adding an *Adagio*, K.546.

Probably the most prolific arranger of his own music after Bach was Beethoven, although some of these arrangements are now said to be spurious. But there are enough genuine ones to show that an arrangement by him usually produced some new idea or a new slant on the music. In one instance, the Octet for wind, Op. 103 (which actually predated his Op. 1), he arranged the work for string quintet, which was published as his Op. 4, and later arranged the Quintet as a trio for piano, violin and cello; this became his Op. 63. His Septet, Op. 20, one of his most popular works in his lifetime, became a trio for piano, violin (or cello) and clarinet, Op. 38, and well worthy of performance in this version. He rewrote the E major Piano Sonata from Op. 14 as a string quartet in F, with certain very interesting differences of layout. In this case, the piano work already had in it a good deal suggestive of a quartet. His least successful arrangement was that of the D major Violin Concerto as a piano concerto! Almost his finest,

I think, must be the piano trio he wrote from the Second Symphony. This is, in every respect, a splendid work, as interesting as its original, and, surprisingly, gives the two string parts music quite independent of their parts in the Symphony. His last outstanding arrangement was of the *Grosse Fuge*, for four hands on one keyboard, published as Op. 134. In this there are some remarkable reconceptions to fit the piano layout, and it is definitely a version for performance as well as study. Tovey once wrote that Beethoven's knowledge of the piano was unfathomable; this arrangement goes far to support that contention.

As to why Beethoven spent time on these arrangements, the primary cause was probably need of money. Furthermore, there was no copyright law to protect his work, and he would obviously wish to forestall others as much as possible.

Dussek transferred the minuet from the third of his three string quartets to the A flat Piano Sonata, Op. 70, *Le Retour à Paris*, in a different key and with a different trio, but one which obviously grew from a similar idea. In this case, too, the music of the minuet, while it is ideal string music of a smooth, *legato* kind, suffered no damage in the transfer to the piano, which was able, in this instance, to use its *sostenuto* in the most effective way. Clementi, it seems, arranged some symphonies as piano sonatas; but since we have not got the symphonic originals, these cannot be assessed. He also arranged a piano concerto which we do possess as a piano sonata, published as Op. 33, No. 3. In this case, interesting as the concerto is, the sonata seems to me to be the gainer.

Mendelssohn arranged the scherzo of his string Octet for orchestra, for one occasion only, and there are three, if not four cases in Brahms's work. The D minor Piano Concerto, Op. 15, began life as a symphony (not completed), became a sonata for two pianos, and then, at Joachim's suggestion (Joachim had already severely criticised the orchestration of the symphony), united the best of both worlds in a piano concerto. The F minor Piano Quintet started as a string quintet, became a sonata for two pianos, and again at last took ideas from both versions to produce the piano quintet. But in both cases the changes and re-arrangements were in fact a search for the right medium. In the case of the orchestral *Variations on the St. Antoni Chorale*, Op. 56, Brahms also made a two-piano work as an equal performing version, with some changes to assist the adaptation. The series of variations which forms the slow movement of the B flat String Sextet, Op. 18, also exists as a piece for piano, which (I believe) predated the sextet. Reger arranged his orchestral *Variations and Fugue on a Theme of Mozart*, Op. 132, for two pianos, very effectively, and again intended as a performing version. But he omitted the orchestral eighth variation, preceding the fugue, and replaced it with a new variation of a totally different character – fast and vivacious where the orchestral eighth is slow and meditative.

There may well be others that I have not called to mind. But with the Schmidt *Chaconne* we are dealing with a work transferred bodily from one medium, one of his favourite instruments, if not his favourite, for which it was conceived, to another, with no change of music, no adaptation of material, some six years after its original conception. I know of only one other instance of this kind, the C sharp minor String Quartet by Pfitzner, also composed in 1925, which later, in 1933, he orchestrated as his First Symphony, again with no change at all in the music. Indeed, in this case, since I have no orchestral score and have never seen one, I have frequently listened to the symphony following the quartet score, and nothing could be clearer. It is the very rare case of a work which goes perfectly in two different media, with no alteration in the music, and in nothing else except what is involved in laying out a large orchestral score from a string quartet.

I cannot say exactly the same about the case of Schmidt's *Chaconne*. He was strongly attracted to the organ, he was himself a good organist, and he added quite a quantity of outstanding music to its repertoire. He was particularly attracted to writing large works for it; indeed, except for the *Four Little Chorale Preludes*, the *Four Little Preludes and Fugues* (not, in fact, so little), the *Weihnachtspräludium und Fuge*, which is in between for size and possibly the most perfect of the shorter organ works, and the chorale preludes on *Der Heiland ist Erstanden* and Haydn's *Gott Erhalte*, the bulk of his organ

music consists of large works, some very large indeed. I have
the greatest admiration for the music, which is as finely
wrought as one would expect from Schmidt in his prime: none
of his organ music was written before 1916. But, with works
such as the *Chaconne*, the huge Prelude and Fugue in E flat, the
Toccatas in A flat and C major, the Fantasia and Fugue in D
major and the Prelude and Fugue in C major I am always
uneasy listening to a performance, for even the finest organists
seem to my ears to be unable to make them clear. I realise that
something depends on the organ used, but this result of lack of
clarity I have found on a variety of organs. It cannot be
merely the extent of the volume, for I have heard many organ
works by Reger in which the volume is at times commensu-
rate, but the music remains clear and does not cause discom-
fort even in not so good performances. In these works of
Schmidt something does not quite come across, *to my ears* (for
no doubt there are others who do not have this difficulty). But
there are two important facts: one is that all the best of the
1924 organ variations on the *Fredigundis* fanfares is already
present in the opera, in some of the greatest orchestral music
ever written, with a clarity which makes it infinitely more
imposing, fine as the organ variations are as a composition.
The second is that Schmidt himself, five years after writing it
for organ, orchestrated the *Chaconne*. So far as I am concerned
it was the wisest thing he could have done. Passages which in
the organ work are always to me a blur of sound are
immediately clear in the orchestral version. They lose nothing
in intensity or grandeur, but one can hear the music. What
prompted Schmidt to make this orchestration I do not know; I
can only say that for me his instinct was right. And I wish he
had done the same for some of the other works I have listed,
especially the E flat Prelude and Fugue.

Everything in the orchestral score, it seems to me, is aimed
at clarity; colour, too, but especially clarity. There are interesting comparisons in layout. Where the organ has single
parts in places the orchestra doubles them at different levels,
but achieves a close approximation to the organ sound. At the
beginning of the $\frac{6}{8}$ section (page 30 in the orchestral score,
page 14 in the organ copy), where the organ's single line

One of the last pictures of Franz Schmidt, taken in Perchtoldsdorf in June 1938. He was already very ill and had another eight months to live.

makes the theme quite apparent, Schmidt gives this line to first violins, but doubles the theme in sustained notes, first on clarinet, then on oboe. On page 39 of the orchestral score, page 19 in the organ version, where the organ has a sustained line, this is played *pizzicato*, divided between second violins, violas and cellos; this is the one place in the orchestral version where a totally different kind of sound is aimed at. One large climax (on page 43 of the orchestral score, bottom of page 20 in the organ copy) is intensified by the addition of rapid demisemiquavers for the orchestra, which do not appear in the organ version.

Apart from such things as these, and there are not many, the orchestral *Chaconne* is a direct orchestrated transcript of the organ work. Much as I love the latter, especially in a very fine recording by Anton Heiller, my own feeling is that the orchestral version gains over the organ almost throughout. The Chaconne, in both versions, will be fully discussed in my second volume, which will deal with all the music involving the keyboard, both piano and organ, chamber, concertante and solo, as well as the two String Quartets.

VII. VARIATIONS ON A HUSSAR SONG
(1930)

There is no question of transcription from any other medium with the *Variationen über ein Husarenlied*, which was conceived direct for the orchestra. There are, however, passages which are a throwback to a work written 27 years earlier, the *Intermezzo* composed in 1902–03, which was later incorporated into his first opera, *Notre Dame*. This is especially true of the slow introduction, and a recalling of part of that introduction later in the work.

It has been claimed that the work is a symphony, in variation form, groups of variations forming the various movements. An examination of the work is enough to dispel this nonsense, remembering, too, Schmidt's own conception of what a symphony is, as shown in his four examples. Ex. 107 gives the theme, following the introduction. This is followed

Ex. 107

(dynamics are different in repeat)

by five variations, five plain statements of the theme, all in the same key, with slight rhythmic divergences and some overlappings with canonic suggestion, but never going beyond suggestion, and with increasing energy in the supporting parts. Throughout the theme is plainly to be recognised; each variation is marked off from the next by a silence. In other words, what we have is a warming-up natural at the beginning of a large set of variations and before the more intricate ones are heard. But nothing remotely resembling the first movement, or part of such a movement, of a symphony. Variation 6 is a beautiful piece of slow *fugato* writing, marked

Lento; No. 7 is an *Andante tranquillo*, Variation 8 is an *Allegretto molto moderato*, No. 9 is simply marked *più tranquillo*, and further develops the material of No. 8. With Nos. 8 and 9 the time has changed to $\frac{6}{8}$. No. 10 is a scherzo-type variation, but short, a development of the tranquil No. 7. It leads to No. 11, marked *Presto*, which is one of the two largest scherzi he ever wrote, the other being the one in the Second Symphony. No. 11 moves straight into No. 12, which is slow and, if No. 11 had been repeated, would have formed a quite characteristic, though unusually brief, Schmidt trio. No. 12 is the last normal variation. What follows is a recalling of the second part of the introduction, leading to a plain statement of the theme, which is varied in its scoring and in certain details, so I suppose it might just pass as a variation. But it is much more like a use of Haydn's habit of stating the theme as a reminder after more complex variations have intervened. This is followed by a huge finale which is, provided it is played uncut (and there are vandals among conductors who do cut it), almost another set of variations in itself. Certainly it provides some of the most exhilarating music I have ever encountered.

Schmidt's variations, which are symphonic though not a symphony, do not anywhere go far from the theme, except in the second part of the introduction. His invention, which is immense in this work, is *round* the theme rather than in the theme, although he does sometimes play ducks and drakes with its rhythm, and at times throws phrases out of gear by imitative false starts. But the work is exciting and exhilarating, even in the characteristic groping beginning of the introduction, with the first part of the theme slowly stammered out brokenly by cor anglais, joined a few bars later by flute and clarinet. The true scherzo, No. 11, begins with a fascinating displacement (Ex. 108) of the sturdy four-beat rhythm of the theme.

If one can pick out one supreme moment from these variations, it would be, for me, Ex. 109, where Variation 11 becomes No. 12, the rapid one beat per bar passing immediately to a six-quaver tempo in which one quaver equals one of the previous *presto* bars. So effective is this that nearly a whole bar of the slow quavers can pass before one realises that

Ex. 108

Ex. 109

the tempo has completely changed.

The Hungarian origin of the Hussar song which Schmidt took for his theme has been queried; it matters little, in fact, what was the origin of this theme. But maybe it was Schmidt's belief that his theme was Hungarian that led him, in the latter part of the introduction, thematically a very distant and twisted version of the second part of the Hussar song, to call on the type of gypsy music that had so pleased Carl Goldmark in the *Intermezzo* from *Notre Dame*, twenty-seven years earlier than the *Variations*. It is this part of the introduction that is recalled following Variation 12.

*   *   *   *   *

I hope I have demonstrated in this first volume the stature of the four Symphonies and Schmidt's importance in a great tradition which, as with all healthy traditions, continues to grow and evolve. Far from the least of the high points in its evolution in this century is Franz Schmidt's contribution.

This ends the first part of my examination of Schmidt's music. Volume 2 will, in due course, consider the five chamber compositions, the piano music (such as it is), the two works for piano and orchestra and the organ music. Volume 3 will deal with the two operas and the oratorio, *Das Buch mit Sieben Siegeln*, showing among other things the organ in another and, for Schmidt, a most important relationship in his work.

Appendix
AUTOBIOGRAPHICAL SKETCH
Franz Schmidt

Translated from the German by Martin Anderson

This essay arose from the endeavour to furnish my future biographer
with information (I am always being asked for biographical material) which to me seems necessary to understand my career as artist
and as human being, and to distinguish these data precisely from
those I do not impart here, since they seem to me thoroughly
unnecessary for such an understanding. I state here clearly and
plainly my wish that said biographer content himself with the facts I
have seen fit to reveal here. I protest especially against any
investigation that aims to uncover further material about my
parents, my childhood, my family life, and similar purely personal
concerns; any subsequent dissemination and publication of such
most private matters, which will contravene my explicitly declared
will, I here term crude and tasteless.

The material which follows, modestly presented here as 'truth
without poetry'[1] is, to the best of my intentions, complete. I expect of
its future editor that he reverently respect the wish I have clearly
expressed above. Further, I would sincerely wish that he tactfully
take the fullest notice of the feelings of persons still alive about whom
I speak quite freely in these lines, which are not intended for
publication, and equally that he respect the feelings of the relatives
who survive such persons.

Earliest Years
1874–1888

I was born on 22 December 1874 in Pressburg (then Pozsony) in
Hungary, which has been Bratislava in Czechoslovakia since the
World War. The house I was born in disappeared long ago. My
father was Hungarian on his mother's side and my mother was
pure-bred Magyar. Both my parents were highly musical: my father

[1] Schmidt's allusion is to Goethe's autobiography, *Dichtung und Wahrheit*
(*Poetry and Truth*), although 'Dichtung' has a much wider sense – almost
'invention'. –TRANSL.

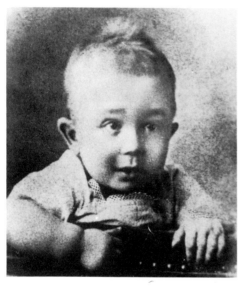

One of the earliest known pictures of Schmidt, who must have been about one year old when it was taken.

used to play different wind instruments, without being able to persevere with any one of them for any length of time, while my mother was an excellent pianist in her younger days[2] and was my first (and best!) teacher.

Music first entered my soul through the church. My first attempts at music, through which my musical gifts came to be noticed, consisted of my playing on the piano the hymns I had heard in church. I was hardly six years old when my mother began to give me regular piano lessons. The piano itself interested me little; all I wanted to do was imitate the organ on it, which I did incessantly.

Since in the long run my mother was unable to give me piano lessons intensively enough, I acquired a teacher. He was one Rudolf Mader, the father of Raoul Mader, who was then Professor of Piano at the Vienna Conservatory and later became Director of the Budapest National Opera. Rudolf Mader taught at the primary school, and his music lessons were unassuming but thorough and conscientious. What impressed me about him above all was that on Sundays he played the organ in the cathedral for the school mass. At this time the Domkirche had just acquired a new and very beautiful organ, the builder of which was the Pressburg organ-builder Vin-

---

[2] Strangely, Schmidt neglects to mention that his mother had been a pupil of Liszt. –TRANSL.

The house in which Schmidt was born can be identified on the right from the name 'Lustig' on the shop front. It is now the site of the headquarters of Slovakian TV and Radio.

zenz Mozsny (a pupil and colleague of many years' standing of Walker in Ludwigsburg). Now, instead of having to stand in row and sing with my class in church, I was allowed to sit on the organ bench next to my teacher. I never tired of bombarding the friendly old man with questions about the nature and construction of the organ. He explained as much as he understood himself and I acquired at least an approximately correct conception of the organ. I was convinced, moreover, that the organ was the grandest and most perfect revelation of music, and it seemed to me that the orchestra, for example, which played an hour later at high mass, was lamentably inferior to the organ. In this particular instance my judgement was fairly accurate, since the organ in the cathedral had a wonderful sound but the orchestra, composed for the large part of amateurs, could barely have been called mediocre.

My lessons with Mader lasted about two years but they had to be given up because of my teacher's illness. After a short interval I obtained a new teacher, Ludwig Burger. Burger, a German national by birth, had found himself in Pressburg as a young conductor to the municipal theatre and, after an ill-considered marriage with a lady from the theatre chorus, had remained in the town. Having long since given up his conducting post, he made a good living in the town as a piano teacher and had a reputation of sorts. Burger was 35 when I became his pupil; he was slender in appearance, with an attractive, characterful head, surrounded with a mane of curly black hair and a thick, full beard; his sharp, pointed nose and his piercing eyes betrayed an unusual temperament.

Unveiled on 19 December 1965, the plaque reads: 'On this spot
stood the house in which was born the renowned composer. . . '.

He began his lessons by declaring Mader to be criminally insane
and starting right at the beginning again with the first five-finger
exercises. For the five years he was my teacher, he swore and
screeched around incessantly. His favourite pose was to play the
part of the neglected German artist, condemned to go to wrack and
ruin in this land of barbarians. It struck me as quite absurd, as his
ability impressed me less and less, and his reputation was much
grander than his accomplishments merited. His teaching methods
were completely without plan; he had me play all sorts of things, all
mixed up, with the result that for me the lesson was fruitless and
remained utterly unenjoyable. Moreover, I felt quite unbeholden to
him and played whatever and however I liked behind the back of my
'teacher', and this is the way that over time I even made real
progress.

By chance I was introduced to the court of Archduke Friedrich[3]
and thereafter had to appear before the public at the wish of
Archduchess Isabella in various benefit concerts of which she was
patron. I created the greatest sensation on all sides. Burger made the
most indescribable scenes, raged and swore, since all this had
happened behind his back, while he was having me play Kuhlau
and Bertini! In view of my successes he finally calmed down and
when even he one day was called to the court as the teacher of some
of the archducal children, he strutted about like a peacock and
swaggered around the town with me appallingly.

In the meantime my father had fulfilled a wish I had long
cherished: he had me learn to play the organ with the young organist

[3] Hapsburg (1856–1937). –TRANSL.

of the Franciscan monastery, Father Felician.[4] With Felician a personality entered my life who was of the deepest and most enduring influence on my entire development as human being and artist. Felician was the complete opposite of Burger: big, strong, blond and infinitely kind – I loved him with all my heart from the moment I saw him. He was not a musician by vocation but had had an academic training as a painter, yet he possessed nonetheless a fundamental knowledge particularly of the theory of music and was an excellent organist, deeply serious about art and religion. His piano-playing, on the other hand, was clumsy and heavy-handed, since he himself never played the piano, although he owned a very lovely new Bösendorfer grand, and thus had me play to him for hours on end and gave me the infinite benefit of his deeply felt and well-reasoned observations on the form and content of the works that had just been played through. Thus I learned harmony and organ with him incidentally and completely effortlessly.

When Burger discovered I was taking lessons with Felician he was furiously angry and gave vent to the most disparaging and spiteful observations; in his opinion he was the only living person to have been called upon to initiate me into the deepest secret of the art of music, but I thank God I was spared that misery! Furthermore, Burger's observation that 'everything the priest teaches is brazen humbug' was given the lie in the most splendid way, in that a few years later, solely on the basis of the knowledge I had gained from Felician, I passed the entrance examination to Bruckner's counterpoint class at the Vienna Conservatory without a hitch, and later too I have never become aware of any gaps or weaknesses in these fundamentals.

I spent all my free time with Felician and he was also useful in my studies at my grammar school – in Latin, for example, I made enormous progress through his help (we held conversations in Latin!). In exchange for this I was to help him with at least the rudiments of the German language, but that didn't get anywhere near success: I couldn't get Felician beyond the most pitiable broken German. The surroundings in which I saw Felician every day were

<hr/>

[4] Tschulik and Nemeth (*op. cit.*) both spell the name 'Felizian'. In *Music in Bratislava* (Orbis, Bratislava, 1978) Zdenko Nováček says something more of the involvement of Mǒik (as he spells the name) in the town's thriving musical life, notably in the establishment of an important children's choir, for which he is commemorated by a marble relief in St. Ursula's Church executed by Augustin Riegele, a prominent local accountant and amateur cellist. – TRANSL.

Schmidt's mother, Maria, *née* Ravasz (1853–1931), photographed around 1926: 'an excellent pianist in her younger days'.

beautiful and exciting at the same time, that is, both the monastery itself, with its brightly radiant pathways and magnificent garden, and its inhabitants, well-educated and lively young men, most of whom belonged to the Hungarian nobility. These young men were quite glad of my presence, for despite my considerable lack of years I was often, and particularly when Felician was away, drawn into skittle parties by them; I also learnt croquet and billiards there – not a fitting diversion for an eleven-year-old, to be sure, but it didn't do any harm. I can, moreover, remember quite precisely: although I always felt much more at home in the company of adults than in that of my contemporaries, I was never what might be called precocious.

What attracted me most, absorbing my every thought and wish, was the organ of this monastery. It was a very old and simple construction by the Pressburg organ builder Klöckner who, as one could read on his sign, was a 'pupil of Silbermann'. Which Silbermann, and whether this was at all true, makes no difference;

its tone was so indescribably beautiful and of such an individual silvery brilliance that I could not tear myself away from it and would spend entire days at this organ. I have never ever found its equal anywhere else. Felician was surely correct when twenty years later he asserted that he could hear that organ throughout my orchestra: the persistent and intensive impression of those sounds in the earliest period of my musical development was surely destined to influence my inner ear for all time.

The specification of the organ was as follows: Hauptmanual– Principal 8′, Gamba 8′, Salicional 8′, Gedackt 8′, Oktave 4′, Spitzflöte 4′, Quinte 2⅔′, Oktave 2′, and Mixtur 5 ranks. Brustpositiv: Copula 8′, Principal 4′, Flauto traverso 4′, Dolce 4′ and Oktave 2′. Pedal: Sub-bass 16′, Violon 8′ and Cello 4′. The 18th drawstop, which was then screwed tight, was that of the former manual coupler which, obviously irreparably rundown, had been taken out long ago; and the organ had never had a pedal coupler. Long after I had left Pressburg around the end of the 1890s, the construction was adapted and enlarged by Mozsny; the addition of several new registers meant that the full work rather forfeited its individual silvery brilliance, but also in this form the organ was one of the finest that I have ever heard.

In the Autumn of 1887 a new acquaintance which took much of my time but which I did not want to go without encroached a little upon my enchanting intercourse with Felician. To this acquaintance I owe all sorts of stimulus, and its influence on me was hardly less than Felician's despite all my resistance. For I was invited one day to the house of an art-loving lady, that of Helene von Bednarics. This lady, no longer exactly young, lived together with an English woman, a friend of hers called Miss Mary Redford, and ran a large house in which there was much music-making. In her large music salon stood two magnificent grand pianos, a Bösendorfer and a Streicher; she also owned a music library which held literally everything that had been written for the piano. The lovely pianos and the music exerted quite a pull on me; but what repelled me was that Fräulein von Bednarics, who gave piano lessons for her own pleasure, wanted without further ado to draw me into her circle of pupils. She had obviously heard much good music and had also read quite a bit about it, for she could talk quite adroitly about music and piano-playing, but since she herself could hardly play the piano at all and thus all her learned chatter hardly impressed me at all – indeed, struck me as highly ridiculous – I staunchly opposed all her attempts to gain musical influence over me. Thus the lady's dearest wish, to be able to regard me as her enthusiastic pupil, was not fulfilled, and thereafter I lived on a war-footing with her. Although I was continually trying to bolt, I didn't manage to stay away entirely; new pretexts were always being cooked up to invite me and with time I even began to feel at ease in this milieu.

Among Fräulein von Bednarics' pupils (all of them young ladies from the best circles in the town) a few were very good. I account for this in that she obviously understood to hold on to people for long-term use, further, that her skilful talkativeness powerfully impressed those creatures who knew no better, and that her method of teaching, stubbornly carried out, could under favourable conditions produce certain tolerable results. With the better of these girl pupils I did a lot of two-piano playing, partly concertos, partly original compositions, partly accompaniment. Thus I learned a huge number of compositions and works that were completely unknown to me. That did me a lot of good compared to the arid one-sidedness of Burger, who some time back had gone over completely to piano-duet playing and threshed me exclusively with Wagner. I certainly don't mean by that that Fräulein von Bednarics wasn't one-sided too. It was that Burger was a rabid Wagnerian: for him there was no music other than Wagner's, apart from a ninth symphony by Beethoven and a Matthew Passion by Bach. By contrast Fräulein von Bednarics was an anti-Wagnerian (there were such things in those days) who was prepared to worship indiscriminately every bit of rubbish beside her chief gods, Schumann and Chopin, but who belched fire and flame at the very mention of Wagner. I abhorred that sort of absurd narrow-mindedness which provoked me to the staunchest opposition, despite my good-natured disposition. All along I was seeking whole-heartedly for people whom I could look up to: I have always bowed in grateful veneration before real authority. My relationship with most of my grammar-school teachers is evidence of this as, more so, is my unconditional devotion to Felician. But it was with the study of music itself that I had the misfortune to deal with really dubious personalities and characters, whose narrow-mindedness provoked my contrariness to the utmost, with the result that, as an impetuous youth, I of course mostly overshot the target. It was no misfortune that Burger's biting scorn about 'the hysterical old hag' brought Fräulein von Bednarics inwardly much closer to me than she herself had ever managed. Solely to annoy Burger I would assert that Jensen's *Pastorale* or Raff's *Polka de la Reine* (the main hit of the musical teas in the Bednarics salon) were magnificent works, and were much dearer to me than boring Wagner with his eternal repetitions. On the other hand I would swear in the Bednarics salon that Bach, Haydn, Mozart and Beethoven interested me solely as preparation for the one true god Wagner and that I ignored everything else written until now as inferior. I never touched Fräulein von Bednarics' piano without striking up Wagnerian chords. Once even, at one of the well-attended musical teas in the Bednarics house, provoked to the utmost by a turn in the conversation, I dashed over to the Bösendorfer piano with a cry of 'This is the music for me!', let rip with the March from Wagner's *Tannhäuser* (in the transcription by Liszt), and would not yield to Fräulein von Bednarics' raging nor to her tears, but still kept threshing away, lovingly and tenderly tickling the poor Bösendorfer until the *Tannhäuser* March was over, the piano badly damaged and I myself half-dead. Well, I am truly ashamed of that sort of excess of contrariness. But when one considers how much my sensitive child's soul was provoked by these stupid people one might perhaps nevertheless find many valid reasons to excuse my behaviour.

Despite all these events Fräulein von Bednarics still hung on to me with a love that was touching, so convinced was she of my unusual gifts, and instead of throwing me out she invited me back again, plied me with the choicest titbits and presented me again and again to new people. All the artists who gave concerts in Pressburg would pass through her salon, which meant all the great names of those days: Anton Rubinstein, von Bülow, Reisenauer, Sarasate, the Hellmesberger Quartet, and many more besides. She presented me to them all and I played to most of them, too. If she had had her way, she would surely have succeeded in launching me, so that I would doubtless already have been a famous pianist as a very young man.

And why did it all happen quite differently? It was just at that time that I had the misfortune to find a pseudo-authority, instead of the personality I was looking for. It happened like this: for me, who was brimming over with enthusiasm and eagerness to learn, and who demanded from myself and all others the highest and best that was possible, for me this person was not the authority I was longing for. Fräulein von Bednarics certainly meant well and can't be held to blame that the man to whom she introduced me was so unsuited to being my teacher that this experience completely threw me off the rails. In January 1888 Fräulein von Bednarics travelled with me to Vienna and brought me before the world-famous pedagogue Theodor Leschetizky.

When I had played to him, Leschetizky's verdict was: 'Astonishingly correct, technically excellent, not enough *charme*'. I had no real idea what he actually meant by '*charme*', but this was yet to become clear to me. After that I travelled to Vienna several times to take lessons with him, but it never came anywhere near being a truly private lesson, for there were always perpetual comings and goings and always two or three young girls, often even more, present, who would listen to my lesson and now and then play themselves. I noticed right at the beginning that Leschetizky wasn't particularly interested in me but had eyes only for the young women, whom he was always fondling and petting, while they for their part would much have preferred to scratch the eyes out of the old fop for his kissing of their hands and similar tendernesses. I also learned in the very first lesson that what was meant by the *charme* that was lacking in my playing was a terrible sort of *rubato* playing, through which compositions were disfigured mostly to the point of unrecognisability and utter meaninglessness; I took comfort, admittedly, in the fact that what was served up in this sugar-water fashion was, for example, Rubinstein, Moszkowski, Schytte and similar rubbish, but occasionally good music too was profaned. Naturally I didn't comply with such 'intentions of the maestro' at all, by which I incurred his utmost displeasure and contempt; he declared me to be slow and ungifted.

Nonetheless I was invited to a 'Wednesday' – it was one of those 'teas' in the Leschetizky household when the maestro's favourite pupils were brought before an invited audience. This Wednesday decided the course of my life. To my greatest surprise, and apparently without having asked the maestro, Madame Annette Essipoff, Leschetizky's wife of that time, called upon me to play. I played Liszt's *Twelfth Rhapsody* and Balakirev's *Islamey* to the frenzied applause of the assembled company. Madame Essipoff showered me with kisses and said lots of pleasant and complimentary things. Leschetizky, who had obviously found the proceedings quite unpleasant, appeared edgy and irritated. He said loudly to the company: 'There's potential there, even quite a lot! But the fellow will never be tidy. Anyway, someone with a name like Schmidt shouldn't become an artist'. This last sentence needs no comment: it is typical of Leschetizky's hatred of everything German, even down to the name. I had long intended, with the agreement of my parents, to discard my father's name because of its frequent occurrence and take up the Magyar name of my mother. This crude statement from the mouth of that odious man was enough on its own to bring to a head the irrevocable decision never to carry out the change in name. Among the many dreadful things that were to be heard on that day I remember with especial horror a performance of the *Wanderer Fantasy* by a young, blonde, English girl and another of the *Appassionata* by an exotic youth from Melbourne. Beethoven and Schubert with caviar, truffles and mixed pickles! So this was '*charme*', 'culture'. That was what he called a 'standard' of pianistic accomplishment. Hopelessly unmusical English girls and Australians were supposed to attain an artistic relationship with Schubert through the maestro's 'interesting' expositions. And this was what they called the Leschetizky 'master class' – this was world-famous!

Shaken with disgust, I left the madhouse buzzing with a Babylonian Babel, with the firm intention of never setting foot in it again. And when I was sitting in the train on the journey home, I came to a decision of great moment: I decided in all earnestness to give up playing the piano completely! The day that had just passed had filled the goblet of disgust to overflowing: these wretched piano people, these Burgers, these Bednaricses, these Leschetizkys – I never wanted to see any of them ever again. I never wanted to touch another piano again. Felician, to whom I opened my heart, at first was very shocked and tried at least to talk me out of the instant execution of my resolution. He also managed to extort from me a promise that I would consider it for a while, with the result that in fact I became a little undecided. But on one point I remained firm: I never again set foot in the Leschetizky household.

What my energy failed to effect thanks to my wavering, fate saw to all the more quickly and fundamentally. A few weeks after the proceedings I have just described above, my parental home fell apart completely.[5] The hopeful child prodigy became a poverty-stricken lad overnight. There was no more talk of further musical studies; it was more a question of overcoming the most pressing worries about food; and thus in the Autumn of 1888 I became tutor to a grammar-school pupil for the price of food and board. I came away from Pressburg, from Felician, from the beloved Franciscan monastery and the lovely organ, indeed, away from Hungary altogether; I came to Perchtoldsdorf, near Vienna, to the Grienauer household.

I endured such a fundamental transformation in my life much more easily than could have originally been hoped, and for a variety

---

[5] Schmidt's rather oblique reference (his obliquity is this time entirely understandable) is more fully explained on p. 26. –TRANSL.

of reasons. Much had been going against me in my home town that made my farewell easier. For example, Frédéric Dohnányi, my physics teacher at the grammar school, who moreover was also my violin teacher, had a son who was all of a sudden brought before the public as a child prodigy of the piano. The first appearance of this prodigy was staged with the most sensational presentation: unusually small for his age, Ernst Dohnányi was passed off as even younger, lifted on to the piano stool after a special contraption had been previously shoved under the piano with much ceremony, and all sorts of such antics beyond that. He was then at most about a year-and-a-half younger than I was; he was in the second and I in the third form at the grammar school when he had his first success at one of the school's festival concerts. I also contributed to this concert, and although I had a big solo number (the Eleventh, I think, of Liszt's *Hungarian Rhapsodies*), while all he played was the easy piano part of Mozart's G minor Piano Quartet, I hardly got a mention in the newspapers while Dohnányi was celebrated as an unparallelled genius. The press abided by this estimation of our relative abilities in the future, too, and although I bore it imperturbably on the outside, it made me extremely bitter within. Another circumstance destined to make my departure from my home town vastly easier was, it must be said, that this departure finally spared me the comings and goings in the Bednarics house, where I had not been able to stand a minute since my break with Leschetizky, for I was unceasingly tormented with reproaches and tears. But the decisive reason that I bore this complete upheaval in my life so easily is that from the first moment I felt so hugely at home in my new environment that I can say with complete justification: one of the loveliest and happiest periods of my life began with my entry into the house of Karl Grienauer in Perchtoldsdorf.

Perchtoldsdorf
1889–91

The Grienauers were a large, rich family, with land in different parts of Lower Austria. In Perchtoldsdorf there then lived three brothers, out of a family of seven brothers and sisters, who had reached different stages in their lives: Ludwig Grienauer, a bachelor, owned the Perchtoldsdorf brewery and some important property; Alois Grienauer was an opera singer, a baritone with the Metropolitan Opera in New York, had just married, and spent his holidays in the

'Grand Villa Grienauer'; and finally Karl Grienauer, the eldest of
the brothers, was the head of the family with which I came to lodge.
He owned the 'Lesser Villa Grienauer' at No. 12 Leonhardsberg and
held a minor post at the North-West Railway Station in Vienna.
Early each morning he would drive off and didn't get back until late
in the evening; accordingly he was virtually never at home, except
on Sundays. It seemed to me that his brothers didn't exactly enjoy
the sympathies of his own family circle; in any case there was a
pronounced antipathy between his wife and his brothers. However
he felt about it, Karl Grienauer was at pains to get on as well with
his brothers as he did with the rest of the world.

Apart from the head of the household, the Grienauer family
consisted of five people: the lady of the house was a very lovable and
lively Viennese lady, if somewhat eccentric and obsessed by an
astonishing prodigality. The eldest daughter, Lotte, was remarkably
well educated but, sadly, in the advanced stages of consumption; her
husband was the violinist Hugo von Steiner, a member of the
Vienna Court Opera Orchestra. A son, Karl, who had just completed his military service, loafed around his parents' house; a
musician by profession, a highly gifted cellist, he was at that time
without a job and thus passed his time practising his cello a little
and turning the girls' heads. A second daughter, Alice, was a quiet,
somewhat morose girl, to whom I never managed to get particularly
close. Finally, the youngest, another son, was Willi, my eleven-year-
old 'pupil', a loafer and scallywag without peer but lovable and
good-natured.

My entry into the Grienauer household had been arranged by
Hugo von Steiner, whom my parents had got to know long
beforehand through his brother Alfons, who had a job in Pressburg.
When Hugo von Steiner first entered my life, the impression he
made on me was of a great artist and a most influential personality.
The first supposition later proved an over-estimation, while the
second was a complete misunderstanding; of course I couldn't have
known then that usually the members of the Court Opera Orchestra
didn't exactly belong among the most influential of people, but his
looks and his brother's grandiloquence brought about this delusion.

My responsibilities in the Grienauer household consisted of
helping Willi, who attended the Jesuit grammar school in Kalksburg, with his homework and giving him piano lessons. We never
put ourselves to any special effort and thus very soon became the
best of friends – hardly surprisingly, given the little difference
between our ages. It never occurred to anyone to keep an eye on us,

and so we had a lot of free time which we spent with the greatest of
pleasure, flying kites or in other ways that were conducive to health.
In my free time I was frequently enlisted in the music-making of
Steiner and Karl Grienauer and thus got to know thoroughly the
complete violin, cello and trio repertoire; and on occasion I was also
used as the second fiddle in the string quartet. Much though this
music-making interested me too, I didn't find complete contentment
in it: Steiner was indeed an excellent fiddler and Karl Grienauer the
younger an extraordinary cellist, but it seemed to me that both
lacked the dedication, the conception of the hallowed nature of the
art which so much inspired me. At least, I found myself a little
strange compared to them but for the time being I held my thoughts
to be exaggeratedly unworldly and eccentric, and I took great pains
to fit in with the playing as well as in appearance, although the latter
always managed to escape me, and I never succumbed to any sort of
light-hearted attitude, which was incessantly working on me
through this intercourse. But these influences did manage to be
decisive in my plans concerning my choice of career. Both of them
honestly meant well when they tried to prove to me that I certainly
had to become a musician but should strike out on completely
different paths and set myself other goals than those I had done until
then: they made the career of conductor out to me as the most
brilliant and worthwhile for me. I should apply myself to studies
that were relevant to it; I could already play the piano more than
well enough, and must not lose any more time! The art of the piano
virtuoso was an unprofitable one (I was disgusted with this judgement made from the point of view of making money); further, it was
an inferior art – of that, to be sure, I had been convinced since
Leschetizky! Both were supported in their arguments by Alois
Grienauer too, who took a lively interest in my future. He, moreover,
had engaged me as a co-repetiteur, whereby I was introduced to the
operatic literature. What interest I still had in the piano perished in
this environment; nonetheless I couldn't decide to study conducting
at the drop of a hat and as a result remained quite undecided for
more than a year about what I ought to begin; indeed, at that time I
was far from certain that I would become a musician at all.

Despite this indecision I wasn't inactive and got down to work on
my grammar-school studies for my own sake, as well as I was able.
Although the Jesuit College in Kalksburg couldn't be compared
with my beloved Franciscan monastery and I found the priests there
quite repugnant, I had nonetheless found a friend and mentor in one
of them. This was Father Hanf, an elderly, erudite man, formerly a

missionary, who had travelled all over the world. He often invited me in and gave me lessons, chiefly in Latin, lent me the books I needed, etc. I feel I owe this distinguished man deep gratitude.

I was busy with something else in deepest secrecy: I was composing. I myself didn't think too much of these attempts and with true appreciation of their worthlessness I have destroyed them all most carefully. But still it would leave me no peace, and I had to keep writing, and if nothing of that remains today it wasn't wasted effort. I must mention here that Hugo von Steiner was also busy composing away: he already had whole piles of violin compositions lying around and at this very moment was writing an opera. The glimpse that I managed to get of his work brought about a fundamental revision of my judgement of his artistic ability. However skilful a violinist he was, he was equally lamentable as a composer: it was the most pedestrian amateurishness then to see the light of day – what he was producing was a thin sugar solution, only, unfortunately, in huge quantities. It was his good luck and others' that he never succeeded in forcing his spiritual children into the public eye; nonetheless these days he kept composing unflaggingly.

I had guarded against showing Steiner anything of my attempts at composition: it would have brought us into sharp opposition. Furthermore, my insuperable attitude to my work was a proud modesty in anything that concerned my work, and even today I find it difficult to decide to let go of a work, indeed, even to admit its very existence.

In those days a matchless miracle, unsuspected by me, was taking place in Perchtoldsdorf: a few minutes away from us Hugo Wolf was living in the Werners' house in the Brunnergasse and composing the *Mörike-Lieder*! Unfortunately I had no opportunity of being presented to him: he lived his life in deep seclusion. Only three times did I see this shy, sombre apparition some way off in the distance on the heath. Moreover, in those days only a very small circle of Hugo Wolf's intimate friends knew of his compositions and were perhaps (?) aware of their eternal greatness; only vague rumours reached us ordinary mortals; we did not experience his divine music until some years later.

Early in 1890, because of unprecedented laziness and a whole series of outrages, Willi Grienauer was expelled from the Kalksburg grammar school. This date is important for me inasmuch as my regular contact with Father Hanf ceased when Willi left the establishment. As a matter of fact, my remaining in the Grienauer household had now become superfluous, since Willi told everyone that no power on earth would ever get him to enter a grammar school or another secondary school. What might become of him didn't trouble anybody very much in this house, where everything was at sixes and sevens, which, like a popular hotel, was constantly swarming with guests, and the head of which, when he was there at all, wandered around like a somnambulist. Nor did anybody think to send me away: I was already pretty well on the inventory, so to speak, and so that I had some claim to stay I was to give piano lessons to Alice as well as Willi. As far as these lessons are concerned, I must confess that they as good as never never took place on account of the continual prevarications of both pupils – which didn't then offend me in the slightest. When I now think that I spent over a year in that house on this pretext, ate myself stupid and did nothing more than amuse myself, I feel implicated in the impoverishment of this uniquely good and kindly family and am racked with somewhat mixed feelings.

The summer of 1890 went by for me like one long holiday: excursions, skittle parties, summer balls, fancy dress balls, in colourful succession. But I wasn't light-headed enough to forget the future entirely: I was turning it over in my head that I had squandered more than a whole year. Since my private grammar-school studies had been rendered considerably more difficult by the cessation of my regular contact with Kalksburg, I decided at least to make a serious attempt in my musical studies at the career of conductor and to enter the Vienna Conservatory in the Autumn. So when the time came I had myself enrolled in Bruckner's counter-point class, and as I was advised that it was completely impractical to put one's name down for a theoretical subject alone, since I could attend it as a second main subject if I chose an instrumental subject, I had myself enrolled without a moment's hesitation for the cello, as for me the piano didn't come into consideration. The violin would naturally have given me more pleasure, but since the Conservatory had violinists 'coming out of its ears', as the Director, Josef Hellmesberger, put it, I would have had no prospect of a free place; still, I definitely needed one of those and thus I became a cellist. To my very great sorrow Bruckner began to fall ill right at the beginning of the school year and so with my colleagues I was moved into the parallel class of Professor Robert Fuchs. But this thoroughly distinguished man and artist was a partisan of Brahms, which was the *casus belli* for us young Brucknerians. Since I didn't want to continue my studies with Robert Fuchs, and Bruckner now couldn't be considered, I left Fuchs' class at the end of the scholastic year and took care of my studies autodidactically. I continued my cello studies, although I was not very interested in them, since I was entirely freed from having to pay for my tuition.

About this time a new upheaval tool place in the circumstances governing my life.

The Grienauers sold their villa on the Leonhardsberg and moved to Vienna. Lotte von Steiner had died, the family was completely impoverished by the excessive spending of the lady of the house and the feasts and revelries that had gone on for years, and had to move into rented accommodation where, faced with ever more wretched circumstances, they then vegetated. So I had to leave the house that had become so dear to me. In the meantime my relatives had moved to Vienna and so I moved in with them and spent the next eight years in my parents' house at 57 Erdbergerstrasse in Vienna.

Further Years at the Conservatory
1891–1896

I can describe the period of my cello studies quite briefly. My teachers on the instrument were: for the first three years Karl Udel, and for the last three years Ferdinand von Hellmesberger. Udel was extremely meticulous and laid a solid foundation. Ferdinand von Hellmesberger's lessons were hardly inspiring and completely inadequate. For an offspring of the Hellmesberger family who had gone his own way, Ferdinand was phenomenally industrious but only moderately gifted and able. He himself practised many hours a day and was capable of repeating each – easy – passage from a string quartet or orchestral work a thousand times. Since he demanded the same of his pupils, he got results in this manner and also had luck with talent, everybody regarded him as a good teacher – on which point I am of a decidedly different opinion.

I had little time to practise my cello; nor did I ever possess a good instrument. My bow and my music were always deposited with the old school attendant Kehlendorfer, and as a rule I went through my exercises a little before the lesson, which for me was easily enough to keep up with the pace of the syllabus. Ferdinard Hellmesberger, who (I think) didn't like me but couldn't find anything to object to in my attainments, one day told my mother, who was inquiring about my behaviour: 'By and large I'm very satisfied. Your son is not exactly gifted, but really very industrious for all that'. I quote this remark verbatim, for it is indicative of the understanding of this teacher for his pupils.

My biggest experience in this year was the 'Theatre and Music Ex-
hibition in Vienna' in 1892, about which I have written a few essays.
I was extremely active throughout my time as a student. I earned
quite a lot of money giving lessons in piano and cello, as a
co-repetiteur with opera and operetta singers, accompanying in
concerts, giving lessons in mathematics, translating from and into
Hungarian,[6] and so on. But I never saved a thing, for I couldn't hold
on to money and would spend it all again immediately.

I continued my grammar-school studies with all sorts of difficul-
ties; from time to time, when necessary, I even took private lessons
in several subjects. In 1893, as a private student, I graduated with
good results from the grammar school in my home town.

My cello course at the Conservatory came happily to an end; in
1896 I passed the leaving examination with excellence and left the
school to take up a post with the orchestra of the Vienna Court
Opera. Ferdinard Hellmesberger was very much astonished that his
'not exactly gifted' pupil, against invited competition from 40
applicants for the Court Opera Orchestra, completely beat the other
39 to win the post.[7]

Therewith ended a rather uneasy and distracted stage of my life,
and now began trouble and bitter disappointments in excess.

Galley Years
1896–1913

When I took up the post in the Court Opera Orchestra on 1 October
1896, I was in truly high spirits: I had achieved the highest goal that
I could reach as a cellist – I had become a member of the Vienna
Philharmonic Orchestra, of the orchestra that Richard Wagner had
called the foremost in the world and I had a job that was safe, even if
it was badly paid. My first turn of duty, *Tannhäuser*, conducted by
Wilhelm Jahn, entirely overwhelmed me. What a huge experience!
What a wealth of impressions! And there were many such feasts:
Fidelio, Tristan, Die Meistersinger under Hans Richter; in addition
there was the emergence[8] of *The Bartered Bride* under Fuchs.

[6] Schmidt's spoken German, whose colour evinced the influence of upper-
class Viennese dialect – the spoken German of the Viennese aristocracy –
didn't show the remotest trace of a Hungarian accent. I was, in fact,
surprised to learn that he knew Hungarian. –HANS KELLER
[7] Documents in the orchestra files put the figure at 14, not 40. –TRANSL.
[8] Schmidt uses the word 'Entstehung', as if to suggest it was a premiere –
which it wasn't. –TRANSL

But soon bitter drops began to fall into my goblet of joy. For there were other conductors there, too, who also waved the baton over me: e.g., Dr Josef Hellmesberger (the younger, for his father had died a few years previously). This man I admired without limit as a violinist of genius but as a conductor he was a highly questionable phenomenon. Talent and ability he had in plenty and his craftsman-like routine was simply perfect, but the casual and frivolous way he dealt with the works he had to conduct was nothing less than outrageous. All he did was beat time, without any sort of nuance, took everything too fast to get it over with sooner and didn't care at all about the singers, who were simply run down by the orchestra which was always playing too loudly.

A still worse example was the conductor and ballet composer Josef Bayer. I compare him, so as not to insult this profession, with a sergeant in an Austrian music regiment only inasmuch as he possessed the gloom and coarseness of one such to the fullest extent. His ability as a conductor and musician would by far have failed the demands of the post of sergeant in a music regiment. He was beneath all criticism, and only the wretchedness and vulgarity of his own compositions were worse than he was. Both these conductors inflicted unhappy hours on me in two ways. It was already harrowing to speak[9] under them; moreover, they had the well-enough known peculiarity of bad conductors in secure jobs of replacing the complete lack of any sort of artistic authority by 'severity'. They found fault in the most wounding way with every least mistake I made and which, given my lack of routine, was hardly a matter for astonishment. Quite in contrast, moreover, to the great conductors who never said anything in such cases or at least held my elder colleagues responsible for not having alerted the newcomer in time of the pitfalls and traps that lay ahead.

And what colleagues! They took it as self-evident that they should deliberately withhold these bits of advice and warnings from me, and they took a childish delight in it if anything accidental happened to me. What kind of a company was this? Wherever I looked, I saw nothing but narrow-mindedness, lack of culture, peevishness, spitefulness, poverty and the proletarian spirit. Not a trace was to be

---

[9] The administration of the Franz Schmidt Haus suggests that Schmidt meant to write '*spielen*' (to play) instead of '*sprechen*' – plausibly, because his spelling and syntax are occasionally quite idiosyncratic, and he did use the wrong word elsewhere (*cf.* notes 8 and 10 to this Appendix). All his 'errors' are noted and discussed in the German edition of the *Autobiographical Sketch* in *Studien zu Franz Schmidt*, pp. 32–34. –TRANSL.

discovered anywhere of even the most superficial interest in the art; they were salaried slaves, who performed their detested work unwillingly and whose sole endeavour was to dispatch it with the least effort! I was dismayed to encounter this in the world's foremost orchestra; now I know that it cannot be otherwise and that only in this way is it possible to serve in an orchestra for years on end. If you approached this task with artistic ambitions you would soon go under. The initial enthusiasm disappears very quickly in the face of the mechanical and restricted nature of the activity, giving way to the phlegm that is as characteristic of orchestral musicians as it is necessary for them. You gradually sink down to the mentality of the coolie, get bored to death night after night, play, as usual, using the least possible energy, and nonetheless form part of the foremost orchestra in the world. And that is the most depressing thing: the recognition that even in the world's foremost orchestra real artistry is not at all required, that purely mechanical precision and safety is the most important requirement and everything else is superfluous and not desired. And as for individual initiative! That is, of course, the worst form insubordination can take. So be warned, young instrumentalists!

After a few months of playing in the orchestra I was so fed up with it that I was firmly resolved to make use of my right of notice and give the post up at the end of the first year of service. But it wasn't to come to that: through the death of Weidinger, my oldest colleague, a post in the Court Orchestra became vacant to which Hans Richter appointed me at once. The post wasn't very lucrative for the moment but guaranteed considerable increases in income in the near future. To relinquish this coveted double post required much reflection, which I gave it, and I stayed.

Early in 1897 Gustav Mahler came to the Vienna Opera Theatre as conductor; half a year later he was its Director. With him came a time of unparallelled stimulus and splendour for the opera orchestra but also a time of constant excitement and anxiety. I don't intend here to embark on detailed praise of the achievements of this remarkable man as director, conductor and composer; I mean to report only how we orchestral musicians experienced him. Mahler burst over the Vienna Opera like an elemental catastrophe. An earthquake of unprecedented intensity and duration shook the entire building from the foundation pillars to the gables. Anything that wasn't very strong had to give way and perish.

In a short time the largest part of the singers fled (Van Dyck, Renard, Reichmann, Winkelmann), conductors (Hans Richter!), two-thirds of the orchestra. In the orchestra in particular Mahler dismissed and pensioned off so many people in his rage that although I was the youngest in 1897, in 1900 I was already the longest-serving active cellist. The principal cellists Hummer and Sulzer, although not formally pensioned off, played now only occasionally, and not at all when Mahler was conducting. Then I had to sit at the first desk, lead and play the solos. Mahler had earmarked me as Hummer's successor to the position of principal, but his intention was most doggedly resisted by his brother-in-law and friend Arnold Rosé. Rosé, as leader, was vested by Mahler with special authority, his use of which was not exactly beyond reproach. He was seized with a sort of Caesar-like madness and ruled in the orchestra with brutal and narrow-minded arbitrariness. His unbearably arrogant behaviour led to the breach with Hummer, who left the Rosé Quartet and later left the opera altogether. Because I was an intimate friend of Hummer, Rosé's hatred and mistrust were transferred to me too. The result was next that, instead of appointing me a member of his quartet as Hummer's successor, as was generally expected, Rosé chose Buxbaum, whose playing in audition had previously been bettered by me and later by others, and who was now engaged in the opera orchestra without anyone else being asked to audition, and to whom Rosé personally guaranteed the position of principal.

The efforts to make me unpopular with Mahler (which was absolutely necessary to make room for Buxbaum) were aided by outside circumstances: by then (1901) I had already had my first success as a symphonist and at this same time Mahler himself was struggling to gain a foothold in Vienna with his symphonies. Since some of the Viennese critics now tactlessly played me off against Mahler, it was an easy matter to suggest to Mahler that I was conspiring against him with the press. But Mahler's estimation of my abilities at first remained unchanged – as usual, whenever he conducted, and without exception, I had to take the first desk. Nonetheless clear signs of a 'fall from grace' could be noticed. Mahler's personal relations with me, in contrast to what they had earlier been, were icily cold. Rosé behaved more loutishly than ever; following the instructions of the almighty leader, the conductors Franz Schalk, Bruno Walter, and others began to greet my solo performances with disapproving, disparaging and spiteful comments. Since I am certainly not thick-skinned,[10] I had a mind to give

[10] Schmidt writes '*Duckmäuser*' ('cringer'); he probably means '*Dickhäuter*' ('pachyderm'). –TRANSL.

up leading, for which, moreover, I had never received the slightest compensation. Naturally, this would have meant abandoning my candidacy for the position of principal once and for all. That would by no means have held me back from taking this step; but I couldn't risk it because it was Mahler's express command that kept me in that position when he was conducting; and at that time he conducted a lot, a good half of all the performances. I had no doubt that Mahler would have dismissed me instantly if I had become obstinate on this point.

Thus this intolerable state of affairs dragged on for some time until one day, while Mahler was away, Rosé made a direct attack. We were performing *Lohengrin*, an opera in which there is no cello solo. Before the performance began I was sitting, as usual, at the first desk when the orchestral attendant brought me orally(!) Rosé's order that I was to remove myself from the first desk, since from now on Messrs Buxbaum and Jeral were going to be sitting at the first desk and were to take it in turns to play the solos. I betook myself to Rosé who was sitting in the orchestra's room and asked him what the reasons for my sudden demotion were and whether I could not have been informed of it in a somewhat more dignified manner. Rosé answered me in his rude, provocative High German: 'I find myself forced to take this step, and you will have to be satisfied with that. I refuse to tolerate any further interrogation'. And in front of all those present he said to the orchestral attendant: 'My order stands. I cannot bear to listen to this man's playing any longer'. I spat in front of Rosé, turned my back on him and immediately reported sick; I was well aware that therewith I was risking dismissal but I was in no condition to play after this scene which had upset me dreadfully.

After a few days, by which time my nerves had calmed down a little, I went back to the theatre and played at one of the back desks. Buxbaum and Jeral, Rosé's two favourites, were both significantly on in years but nonetheless considerably younger than I was in years of service. They found themselves in a very difficult position through their ponderousness and uncertainty, for when Mahler conducted, knowing that they had been forced upon him by Rosé, they were especially anxious and completely failed as leaders. In my bitterness about the shabby treatment that had been meted out to me I was not at all inclined to help out, although I knew exactly what the position was. Thus there were continual misunderstandings and when they changed over Mahler gave a disapproving shake of his head. The two unlucky leaders were getting more and more nervous and despondent, since they could not help but notice Mahler's manifest disapprobation of their abilities. One morning, after repeated, thoroughly embarrassing accidents Mahler, who was to conduct *Die Walküre* that evening, notified me during rehearsal that I was to play the solos in the evening. I hurried to his office and had myself announced. I was admitted at once and explained that I was prepared to lead and play the solos in *Die Walküre* that evening if I was given the permanent contract for the position of principal there and then. I also complained about the unauthorised demotion Rosé had ordered. Mahler leapt up and shouted at me: 'What do you mean? Are you setting me conditions? Are you trying to play hard to get?' He continued in this tone; when I could get a word in, I pointed out that I could not see with what right the Opera should demand of me that for years I should do a more highly qualified job than I was contractually required to do without the slightest thought of compensating me in any way. Pale with rage, Mahler bellowed at me: 'You! I am at the end of my patience! You be careful! If you refuse to play for me, or say one more word, you can consider yourself dismissed! I'm warning you!'

I bowed and left. Mahler's warning rang in my ears all day long, but nonetheless I decided to push matters to the limit and not to give in whatever happened. That evening I went into the theatre earlier than usual and sat down at the last desk. Neither the official order brought to me by the orchestral attendant nor the brutal threats Rosé personally hurled at me could persuade me to exchange my seat for the principal's; and so, like it or not, Buxbaum had to sit at the first desk since Mahler could already be heard approaching and everybody had to be sitting in place when he stepped on the podium. Mahler surveyed the situation with a single glance; he didn't turn a hair. The performance began and came to an end. Mahler said nothing, but I wasn't dismissed.

After I had officially given up the fight for the position of principal through my 'refusal to play', I vegetated for fully ten years more in the Vienna Court Orchestra; as a '*homo suspectus*' it wasn't exactly a bed of roses, but at a comfortable distance from the hotly contested post I was left in relative peace from now on. During these ten years the filling of the cello post remained an unsolved problem. All sorts of experiments and all sorts of people were constantly being tried, partly from our ranks, with whom the method was promises one minute and threats the next, and partly with cellists summoned from abroad. Thus there cropped up for a shorter or longer time the names Krasselt, van Vliet, Herkenraat, etc., although not one of them was suitable and they all departed once more. One rather longer and very promising episode was the engagement of the Dutchman Willem Willeke. If they had understood how to hold on to this young artist, Vienna would once again have had a cellist of the very foremost rank, who would have brought the cello in the world's leading orchestra back to its former glory. But Willeke wasn't sufficiently devoted to the power-crazed Rosé; he was thus abused for so long that it became too much for him and after playing for barely two years of service he upped and left. Willeke then obtained much honour and wealth in America as the cellist of the famous Kneisel Quartet.

How the problem of the principal cello position was solved after my departure – indeed, whether any satisfactory solution was found – I do not know. Buxbaum and Jeral both referred to themselves as 'Principal Cello of the Vienna Court Opera Orchestra'; whether one of them actually attained the position, or whether both were simply jollied along for further years with promises and fibs is beyond my pen. I have depicted my experiences in the struggle for the position of principal cello so exhaustively because the whole procedure seems to me to be a thoroughly instructive example of how artists are treated in the orchestra – even in the best in the world.

After Mahler had become entirely exhausted as Director, Felix Weingartner followed him onto the throne. His directorship was unable to eliminate the confusion in which Mahler had left the establishment but instead appeared much more likely to increase the chaos yet further. Coupled with a most serious artistic decline the financial deficit had grown to an unprecedented size. To overcome the latter grievance at the outside, the management of the Court Theatre had now decided to appoint a tried and tested man of the theatre to the directorship, even if he wasn't a prominent musician, and they believed they had found such a person in Hans Gregor from Berlin. Gregor, an actor by profession, was a brilliant director and a seasoned businessman who was used to managing his own theatres which he had to make profitable if he was to avoid penury. These abilities, as well as his nerve, which was quite unknown in these parts (he had once been a Prussian officer), would have put him in a very good position to bring order to the desolate conditions of the Vienna Opera if – unfortunately – he hadn't been completely unmusical. Thus he was dependent in all musical matters on the information of those of his subordinates who knew about music. He had surrounded himself with a staff of 'artistic directors' who weren't chosen from any particular viewpoint other than that he could leave them to their duties, just as he found them, and increase their authority while he concerned himself exclusively with the stage. One can well imagine how these subalterns, who had now become 'directors', took to their generals' uniforms. If Rosé had had to submit to some limitation of his authority under Mahler and Weingartner, at least with respect to artistic matters, he now began to establish unrestrained protectionism.[11] The other artistic directors behaved in exactly the same way in their departments, and it is thanks only to the circumstance that the directors constantly got in one anothers' way and thus at least kept themselves in check that the opera orchestra was not entirely ruined during this period. No day went by when I would not have considered fleeing this artistic hell. I had had a position in the Conservatory of the Gesellschaft der Musikfreunde since 1902. When this establishment was taken over by the state in 1910, becoming the Academy of Music and the Performing Arts, and in 1912 my professorship of cello there was changed into a piano chair, my material position became so much better compared to what it had been formerly that I could now dare to make the move.

What gave me the final shove to execute this long-cherished plan was that Hans Gregor had taken on the premiere of my opera *Notre Dame*. I do not intend to tell the sorrowful tale of this work, which was written in the years 1902 to 1904 but which was not performed until 1 April 1914. For the moment only this much: Gregor had accepted the work for his Berlin theatre solely on account of the libretto since he could form no opinion of the music for himself, but through his appointment to the Vienna Opera he had been prevented from producing it in Berlin. He brought *Notre Dame* with him from Berlin to Vienna and put the work in his Vienna programme right from the very beginning. But he needed all of two years to overcome the resistance of his artistic directors and to carry out his plan; only Franz Schalk, for his part, spoke up for the work. When the performance contract had been signed, I regarded the time as come to give up my duties at the opera and to fall back on the piano

[12] The rift between Schmidt and Rosé was eventually to be healed. Hans Keller's 'Personal Recollections' refer (p. 8) to Schmidt's playing with the Rosé Quartet; and, indeed, he played both piano with Rosé and cello with his Quartet on more than one subsequent occasion. Furthermore, the photograph on p. 143 would seem to indicate some degree of cordiality between the two men. But the most convincing evidence that relations improved substantially is in the dedication in 1929 to Rosé of Schmidt's Second String Quartet, in G major. –TRANSL.

professorship at the Academy. I had already left the Court Orchestra and Philharmonic Union previously since conditions in them had long since become unbearable, and so I cast off the job in the opera orchestra without regard to material issues (the pension) and stopped being a cellist once and for all. Indeed, I was very well aware that the piano chair would give me just as little artistic satisfaction as my orchestral post. But I was just as well aware that it was essential that I left the orchestra if I wanted to be taken seriously as a composer. Why a lion of the keyboard and professional producer of piano-thumpers should be more highly valued by the public than a player in the Philharmonic is quite beyond my comprehension, but it is unfortunately an irrefutable fact. I can mention a grotesque experience as a dramatic example of the correctness of this assertion. In the salon of a rich and clever (if not over-cultured) lady I was always asked, impulsively, if I would play the piano, and when I sat at the instrument I was kept at it for hours. I didn't mind playing there, since both the lady of the house and the friends who gathered round her I found surprisingly pleasant thanks to their genuine interest in and healthy feeling for music. At one of these musical soirées, after I had performed various operatic fragments as well as a series of representative works from the piano literature, the lady of the house cried out enthusiastically: 'It's an eternal shame you didn't become an artist!' 'What do you mean, madam?' I asked, embarrassed; whereupon came the answer: 'Well, you are unfortunately not an artist by profession, but simply a musician in the opera orchestra!'

Epilogue

Now, at last, I was no longer an orchestral musician and could hope to commit, if I managed, a healthy amount of my past life to oblivion and with time gain public esteem as an 'artist'. Whether and how I managed my contemporaries and successors must decide.

I consider the continuation of this autobiographical sketch superfluous. Since the premiere of my Second Symphony (3 March 1913) and of my opera *Notre Dame* (1 April 1914) I have been fully in the public eye, and anyone interested is at liberty to discover and inform himself of my works and of my artistic destiny by personal enquiry or by reading up specialist literature, newspaper reports and the like.

In the preceding essay I have assembled for my future biographer the material that is hardest to obtain, namely, that which occurred before I become publicly known. I have already established at the beginning that my wish was not only to facilitate therewith the task of said biographer but also to draw certain lines with regard to the sketch of the part of my life described above. Any infringement of those lines would be utterly against my express wish. Trusting in the respect and tact of my unknown collaborator I leave behind these notes. They are a plain, simple report.

Truth without Poetry

BIBLIOGRAPHY

This bibliography contains references that either are general or deal specifically with the music discussed in the first volume of this three-volume series. The two which follow will each carry a specialised bibliography – although regrettably all three will be very short (and a list containing solely English references would have been barely two lines long). An earlier bibliography appears in: HELGA HAUPT, 'Verzeichnis des Schrifttums über Franz Schmidt', *Musikerziehung*, Vol. 8, No. 3, March 1955.

The first two entries in the following list are useful collections of articles on Schmidt, the first being a commemorative publication on the centenary of his birth.

ELISABETH LAFITE (ed.), *Sonderheft Franz Schmidt (1874–1939), Österreichische Musikzeitschrift*, Volume 29, No. 11, November 1974.

OTTO BRUSATTI (ed.), *Studien zu Franz Schmidt*, Universal Edition for the Franz Schmidt Gemeinde, Vienna, 1976.

JOSEF DICHLER, 'Franz Schmidt – der Mensch', *Österreichische Musikzeitschrift*, Vol. 9, No. 12, December 1954.

J.B. FALKNER, 'Symphonie oder Oper?', *Austria Musikkurier*, December 1949 – January 1950.

ERICH GRAF, 'Franz Schmidt and his Fourth Symphony', sleeve-note to Decca recording, SXL 6544, London, 1972.

ALFRED JIRASEK, *Erinnerungen an Franz Schmidt* (ed. M.J. Jirasek), Leykam Verlag, Graz, 1975.

HANS KELLER, 'Natural Master', *The Listener*, Vol. 112, No. 2881, 25 October 1984.

KARL KOBALD, 'Franz Schmidt, der Mensch und Lehrer', *Österreichische Musikzeitschrift*, Vol. 4, January–February 1949.

PAUL-GILBERT LANGEVIN, *Le Siècle de Bruckner, La Revue Musicale*, Nos. 298–299, Éditions Richard Masse, Paris, 1975.

ANDREAS LIESS, 'Der letzte österreichische Klassiker: sein Leben und Wirken', *Österreichische Musikzeitschrift*, Vol. 4, January – February 1949.

———, *Franz Schmidt – Leben und Schaffen*, H. Böhlaus, Graz, 1951.

ALOIS MELICHAR, *Die Unteilbare Musik*, Weinberger, Vienna, 1952.

CARL NEMETH, *Franz Schmidt: Ein Meister nach Brahms und Bruckner*, Amalthea Verlag, Zurich, 1957.

——, 'Ein neuaufgefundenes Skizzenblatt zu Franz Schmidts *Variationen über ein Husarenlied*', *Österreichische Musikzeitschrift*, Vol. 12, No. 9, September 1957.

ZDENKO NOVÁČEK, *Music in Bratislava*, Orbis, Bratislava, 1978.

ERICH SCHENK, 'Der Ehrendoktor Franz Schmidt', *Musikerziehung*, Vol. 9, No. 1, September 1955.

ROLAND TENSCHERT, 'Franz Schmidt', *Zeitschrift für Musik*, February 1952.

HAROLD TRUSCOTT, 'Franz Schmidt: Symphonist', *Monthly Musical Record*, Vol. 86, No. 977, September–October 1956.

——, 'Franz Schmidt (1874–1939)', *The Symphony*, Vol. 2: Elgar to the Present Day (ed. Robert Simpson), Penguin, Harmondsworth, 1967, rev. edn. 1977.

NORBERT TSCHULIK, *Franz Schmidt – A Critical Biography*, Glover & Blair, London, 1980.

INDEX

Volumes 1 and 2 will carry individual indices, and Volume 3 a cumulative index to all three books in the series.